100 LIFE GOALS

**A Step by Step Guide for Designing Your Life
and Living with No Regrets!**

Brian Klodt

10-10-10
Publishing

100 Life Goals
A Step by Step Guide for Designing Your Life and Living with No Regrets!
Copyright © 2018 Brian Klodt

ISBN-13: 978-1727154450
ISBN-10: 1727154452

Limits of Liability and Disclaimer of Warranty
The author and publisher shall not be liable for your misuse of the enclosed material. This book is strictly for informational and educational purposes only.

Warning – Disclaimer
The purpose of this book is to educate and entertain. The author and/or publisher do not guarantee that anyone following these techniques, suggestions, tips, ideas, or strategies will become successful. The author and/or publisher shall have neither liability nor responsibility to anyone with respect to any loss or damage caused, or alleged to be caused, directly or indirectly by the information contained in this book.

Medical Disclaimer
The medical or health information in this book is provided as an information resource only and is not to be used or relied on for any diagnostic or treatment purposes. This information is not intended to be patient education, does not create any patient-physician relationship, and should not be used as a substitute for professional diagnosis & treatment.

Publisher
10-10-10 Publishing
Markham, ON
Canada

Printed in Canada and the United States of America

Contents

100 Life Goals

A Step by Step Guide for Designing Your Life and Living with No Regrets!

Personal Development
1 Read (Study) self-help
2 Define your core values
3 Attend self-help seminars
4 Develop a power hour
5 Find a mentor
6 Learn continuously
7 Develop your positive attitude
8 Develop your communication skill
9 Write your life purpose
10 Discover your spirituality

Health and Fitness
15 Eat healthy
12 Maintain you ideal body weight
13 Be aerobically fit
14 Be strong - lift weights
15 Develop a calm mind
16 Learn to prepare healthy meals
17 Learn self defence
18 Complete an endurance event
19 Play a sport(s)
20 Develop a long-life mindset

Family and Friends
21 Choose good friends
22 Find your life partner
23 Treat your partner as a VIP
24 Go out on regular date nights
25 Learn how to be a good parent
26 Be there for your children
27 Have regular family meetings
28 Establish annual family traditions
29 Be a good friend
30 Be a good Son, Daughter, Sibling

Financial
41 Learn personal finance 101
42 Learn to manage your money
43 Develop a budget
44 Develop a good credit rating
45 Track & develop your networth
46 Invest 10% of your income
47 Find a financial adviser / mentor
48 Own investment real estate
49 Increase your income
50 Plan your retirement

Career
51 Do a career assessment
52 Get an education
53 Find or develop your passion
54 Join a professional association
55 Be a good employee
56 Be a good leader
57 Be an expert in something
58 Become an authority
59 Be your own boss
60 Create multiple income sources

Adventure
61 Take a family driving adventure
62 Go to a themepark(s)
63 Animal adventure(s)
64 Go on a camping trip(s)
65 Take a land adventure(s)
66 Take an air adventure(s)
67 Take a water adventure(s)
68 Take an underwater adventure(s)
69 Create your own adventure
70 Climb a mountain

Travel
71 Take a staycation
72 Travel in your own country
73 Attend a major sporting event
74 Attend a major cultural event
75 Visit one of the 7 Wonders
76 Enjoy an all-inclusive vacation
77 Take a cruiseship vacation
78 Go on an island vacation
79 Go to an entertainment city
80 Travel the world

Lifestyle
81 Eat at great restaurants
82 Declutter your life
83 Take weekend getaways
84 Buy high quality stuff
85 Buy your first house
86 Experience life
87 Own a vacation property
88 Pay others to do chores
89 Drive your dream car
90 Live in your dream house

Giving Back/ Legacy
91 Keep a life journal
92 Make a difference in the world
93 Donate to charities
94 Volunteer in your community
95 Trace your ancestry
96 Prepare your will
97 Write a book
98 Document your life story
99 Be a philanthropist
100 Leave a financial inheritance

Hobbies and Passions (Life Goals 31-40)
Acting, Animal Care, Automotive, Billiards, Boating, Bowling, Cars, Church, Computers, Concerts, Crafts, Curling, Dancing, Designing, Entertaining, Equestrian, Fishing, Games, Gardening, Golfing, Hiking, Home renovations, Interior decorating, Mortorcycles, Movies, Music, Painting, Pets, Photography, Reading, Religion, Sewing, Skiing, Spirituality, Swimming, Tennis, Travel, Volunteering, Yoga . . . and hundreds more

Choose 5, 10, 50 or more from this list of top 100 recommended goals to live out your best life.
Create your own list after reading the 100 Life Goals book.

This book is written for people, of all ages, looking to achieve more in life by writing down and achieving their goals.

I dedicate this book to my wife, Kathy, and my children, Karah and Maddie, the most important people in my life, and who have contributed greatly to the writing of this book and living out our life adventure.

FOREWORD

Have you been searching for more purpose? Are you living the life you want? Do you have written goals? Imagine what it would be like to live so that you can say at the end of your life, "WOW, I can't believe all I've accomplished!"

If you are seeking to live a good life, Brian Klodt's book, *100 Life Goals*, is for you! Taking goal setting to a whole new level, Brian has developed one of the most comprehensive goal setting systems I've ever seen, with 100 perfectly designed goals across 10 areas of life, all critically important to living a great life, including goals with Personal Development, Health and Fitness, Family and Friends, Hobbies and Passions, Finance, Career, Adventure, Travel, Lifestyle and Leaving a Legacy.

Brian is proof that by reading, studying and acting on the recommendations of some of the greatest inspirational leaders in the self-help industry, you too can design a life that you are proud of. A student of success principles for the past 25+ years, Brian has gone on to own an entire street of homes, become a multi-millionaire, be an accomplished musician, have a professional career and most importantly, have a loving family life with his wife Kathy while raising two beautiful and accomplished daughters.

Whether you choose just a handful of these goals to accomplish for yourself, or you commit to accomplishing all 100, this book will inspire you to write them down and live a life with purpose. This guide provides a place for you to record your goals, your first step to goal accomplishment. As an added bonus Brian has developed a program at www.100GoalsClub.com to help you stay focused and motivated to achieve your goals. I recommend you read this book, write down your goals and commit to fulfilling them to live your own best life.

Raymond Aaron
NY Times Bestselling Author

ACKNOWLEDGEMENTS

Thank you to my wife, Kathy, who has been a wonderful partner and wife for the past 25+ years as we navigate through this journey called life.

Thank you to my daughters, Karah and Maddie, for having grown into such great young adults; I am proud to be their father (or Daddy, as Maddie still calls me)! Thank you to my parents, who provided me a solid foundation of values. To my father, Morley Klodt, who passed away at age 83. He was a hard-working man who drove an oil truck and rototilled gardens, lived a health-inspired life, and tended to his organically grown tomatoes, decades before organics was popular. My mother, Gunnell Klodt, is a strong example of someone who loves life and is socially active within her retirement home. She dedicated her life to helping my sister and I succeed.

Thank you to my sister, Laura, and her children, Blake and Emily, for being so supportive to our parents and my family throughout our life. May we continue to make great family memories together.

Thank you to my wife's family, starting with Joe and Aurella, the best father-in-law and mother-in-law a marrying spouse could hope for; and to the entire family—one of the closest families I know of—Brenda, Cassie, Brittney; Nancy and Dale, Brianne and Alex, Charlotte, Sherrill and Dylan; Noela, Tyler, Marcella and Mike, Violet, Theo.

Thank you to my best friend, Gary Shaw, for being such a positive influence in my life, and for having opened the door to so much that is good in my life. And to his wife Sue, and their children, Kelsey, Connor, and Katelyn, who have been part of this wonderful journey together. Kathy and I enjoy our friendships immensely.

Thank you to Howard and Mary, great friends of ours. If I ever need someone to teach a course on good parenting, I will be calling upon them as role models.

Thank you to Gary and Donna, a couple we met through our daughters competing on the Canadian National Rhythmic Gymnastics team, with whom we've become lifelong friends and are travelling the world with.

Thank you to my employer for over two decades of meaningful employment and wonderful people. There are so many people I've known over the years, whom I'd like to acknowledge—some who have since moved on—especially Mike (who hired me back in 1991), Mark (former President), Al (former President and inspirational leader), Paul (my boss for more than 15 years), Roman (VP HR), Brian (former boss), and my Bid and Proposal team, led by Terry and Dan. A special thanks to Graham, who has been such a remarkable Proposal Manager for the last 15 years.

Thank you to my Karate Sensei, who was the most influential mentor during my early years, for teaching me so much more than Karate.

Thank you to some great musician friends who have made and played some great music together, performing in several bands over the years; namely: Tim Park, Kevin Coates, and Paul Rose, from the band, *Dorian Wild*, with whom we still perform for special occasions. And also, to their lovely wives Linda, Nan and Rox.

To my lifelong high school buddies, Paul Celi, Dennis Hayes and Brad Levey, for being good friends for so many years, and for our shared love of music.

Thank you to Dr. Christopher Cooper and Jamie Stowe for their magnificent work done to restore our Gables on the Park properties. They are true craftsmen, and people devoted to the preservation of heritage properties. Thank you to Ramona for providing the guidance and inspiration to transform our interior and exterior spaces, and for giving us the confidence to move forward with key design decisions.

Thank you to the magnificent coaches who inspired our children to excel in their respective sports: Jennifer Galijet (rhythmic gymnastics coach), and James Parish (equestrian coach), who taught our children many life lessons along the way.

Thank you to my Toastmasters mentor, Dave Howlett, for inspiring me to be a better speaker and person. He has created a remarkable business around being a

Real Human Being (RHB) and speaks professionally to organizations across this country.

Thank you to Tom and Nick Karadza, of Rock Star Real Estate, for providing such an inspirational investment club for real estate investors and those interested in entrepreneurial training and personal development, to "Live Life on Your Terms", inspiring me greatly over the last decade. To our Rock Star coach, Mike Desormeaux, for helping guide our most recent real estate transactions.

Thank you to the many mentors from the self-help field—I've read their inspirational books and listened to their audio tapes over the years (Yes, this pre-dates CDs and podcasts.): Jim Rohn, Brian Tracy, Dennis Waitley, Steven Covey, Les Brown, Tony Robbins, Robin Sharma, and so many others.

And finally, thank you to Raymond Aaron for this wonderful opportunity to publish my book through his 10-10-10 program, and provide meaningful mentorship through his Monthly Mentor program. And a special thank you to Barbara Powers, my book architect.

LIFE GOALS

Long-term goals are what make up the *dreams* for your life. This book focuses on long-term life goals. Throughout my life, I've been an avid goal setter, having written and re-written hundreds of goals, and doing my best to achieve them while raising a family and having a full-time career. I am a better person and have accomplished more in my life as a direct result of having written goals. One of my 100 goals set at the age of 30 was to write a book. These goals are written with deep reflection about living a life with no regrets; and they represent goals that I believe could be of interest to a wide range of people, as a *template* for designing a good life. This book will benefit . . .

- High school students looking to establish their career
- Graduates who have completed their studies and are looking for their first job(s)
- People in their twenties who are looking for direction in their life
- People in their thirties, with young families, who are looking for more purpose
- People in their forties who are taking stock of their aspirations for the balance of their career
- People in their fifties who are starting to think about retirement goals
- People in their sixties who are planning their retirement and thinking about their bucket list
- People of any age who are looking to take their life to the next level
- Anyone and everyone else who is wondering, *"What is my purpose in life?"*

Each of the 100 goals start out as a *Goal Area,* which is provided as a guide to develop your own, more specific goals by adjusting them to apply to your own life. Suggested goals are provided. Many of these goals are lifelong goals, such as *Develop a Positive Attitude,* where the goal is to develop and maintain a positive attitude for the rest of your life.

Embedded within some of these 100 goals are life habits. These habits are so important to your long-term happiness, health, and wealth that I've included them as goals. Once learned and applied consistently, they will help you achieve the balance of your 100 goals. The goals that are habits to be developed as a result of setting a goal, include:

1 – Read self-help
3 – Attend personal development seminars
4 – Develop a power hour
6 – Learn continuously
11 – Eat healthy
12 – Maintain your ideal body weight
13 – Be aerobically fit
14 – Be strong (lift weights)
15 – Develop a calm mind
23 – Treat your partner as a VIP
26 – Be there for your children
46 – Invest 10% of your income (pay yourself first)
49 – Increase your income
55 – Be a good employee
82 – Live a decluttered life
86 – Have a wide range of experiences
91 – Keep a journal

No two of us are alike, but the fundamentals of living a good balanced life are universal. We all want to be the best we can be: to be healthy, to have good relationships, to have a sense of adventure, to have a rewarding career, to make money, to travel, to have a good lifestyle, to leave a lasting legacy. If some of these goals don't inspire you, don't write them down. But my hope is they will inspire you to think of other goals that do inspire or excite you. There is value in looking at real tangible lists of goals that others have set in their life, to stimulate your own thought process. The goals are across 10 areas of life, all critically important to living a great life, including goals with Personal Development, Health and Fitness, Family and Friends, Hobbies and Passions, Personal Finance, Career, Adventure, Travel, Lifestyle and Giving back/Legacy. I provide suggested goals; and I leave space for you to come up with and write down your own goal for each of the 100 life goals. The book presents suggestions for both *Target* goals and *Outrageous* goals. Outrageous goals are meant to stretch your mind as to something that would be amazing for you to achieve, but not necessarily something you think you are prepared to commit to now. You don't need to feel stress about not achieving an outrageous goal.

I wrote this book for 3 reasons:

1. This was one of my 100 goals, written at age 30, in the category of Father; to create a legacy for my children, and leave behind words of wisdom and guidance for their life, should they need it.
2. To hold myself accountable for living the life I've dreamed and am yet to fully live (Approximately 20% of these goals, I have yet to fully achieve.). See MY GOAL TRACK RECORD, **page 171.**
3. To teach important life skills, and help as many other people as I can to write down and begin working on their own *100 Life Goals.*

This book can be used as a reference book, to be revisited often (minimum annually) and throughout the course of your life. Be a long-term thinker.

DESIGNING YOUR LIFE

What They Didn't Teach You in School

Most of us have had some amazing teachers in our lives; some have inspired us to be better students and human beings. Many of us, however, end up having graduated from secondary school, or beyond, and realize that there are things in life that we wish were taught to us at school. Why are some of the most important things, which are required to live a successful and happy life, not formally taught to us?

- How to handle and manage money
- How to develop exceptional verbal communication skills
- The importance of developing a lifelong habit of daily exercise and eating sensibly
- The importance of setting goals in your life and how to design the life you want
- The entire field of self-help and personal development
- Career planning
- Starting a business or developing multiple streams of income

One of the greatest problems with our educational system is that the importance of goal setting is not even taught, yet it is one of the most important life skills. Entire generations of families grow up and never understand goals or the importance of writing them down.

For every level of our school system, starting with primary school, wouldn't it be great if a course was offered on Life Skills, starting with Life 101, and progressing to Life 102, 103, 104, etc., as we move through our educational system.

Recommended course topics to include:

- Thinking positive
- Exercise daily
- Set goals (or 100 life goals)
- Make money work for you (compounding, investing in stocks and real estate, developing multiple sources of income)
- Read a book a month (keep learning)
- Find a mentor/coach
- Communicate well
- Do things you love
- Keep a journal
- Associate with good people

Some of us are fortunate to have been raised by parents who already have these important skills, and are more successful as a result. For many others, I suspect this is not the case, as our parents have been raised by the same educational system. Some of us are fortunate, as I was, to find a mentor who inspired me to learn about these areas. In my case, my first mentor was my Karate Sensei. I started training in my early 20s, with a Sensei who taught me so much more than Karate; he taught me many of the things I mention above. He was running a course for his students, called Improve Your Life, which, for most of us in his classes, was our introduction to personal development and how to design a good life. Goal setting was taught and encouraged. Striving to be a good and better person was expected, in addition to learning how to kick and punch. Who would have guessed that these kinds of life skills would be taught by a Karate teacher! It was here that I also learned an important mantra, which I would say daily for the rest of my life. After attending one of his seminars, I came away with the expression that has been forever engrained in my mind, and I repeat often . . . "I am Happy, Healthy, Wealthy, and Wise."

I've talked to many people over the years who also recognize the deficiency with the content of what is being taught at schools. Changing an educational system, however, is currently beyond what any of us can achieve on our own. Throughout the course of my last 20 years, I've often thought about how great it would be if there was a franchised place to go for students to learn these essential life skills, accompanied by a fitness or sporting program to help them improve their fitness and energy level.

One of the reasons I've written this book is to help our younger generation of students realize that there are places and strategies on how to live a greater life with more purpose . . . a life that we can look back on and say, **"WOW, what a life!"** This book is written to help you design your life with no regrets, one goal at a time! It is my goal to further accelerate this learning through my website, **www.100GoalsClub.com**, by providing a place people can go to intimately share their goals, both successes and failures, providing encouragement along the way.

Definitions of Success

We all want to be successful. But what is success? The term, *success*, can mean many things to different people, including a view of one's achievements in business, income levels, happiness levels, overall attitude and outlook towards life, personal growth, and much more.

From a prominent on-line dictionary, success is defined as:

1. Achievement of an action within a specified period of time or within a specified parameter. Success can also mean completing an objective or reaching a goal.
2. Colloquial term used to describe a person that has achieved his or her personal, financial, or career goals.

Achieving success in life is so much more than achieving financial or business success. Success is a journey and not a destination to get to. It's important that you develop the mindset that you feel happy and fulfilled along the way while in pursuit of your goals, not just when you've achieved them.

I hope that if you're not feeling successful yet, that within the next year you will be able to confidently feel that you are living a successful life. I can positively say that I believe I've achieved success in my life, and if I were to die tomorrow, I'd have few regrets. For me, making forward progress in each of the 10 goal areas in this book is my indicator for whether I'm successful.

Following are some amazing quotes about success, which are seriously worth studying. Success is . . .

"The progressive realisation of a worthwhile goal or dream."
~ Paul J. Meyer

"An inner feeling of happiness, accomplishment, and self-worth."
~ Source Unknown

"Success is best measured by how far you've come with the talents you've been given."
~ Anonymous

"To laugh often and much; to win the respect of intelligent people, and the affection of children; to earn the appreciation of honest critics and to endure the betrayal of false friends; to appreciate beauty; to find the best in others; to leave the world a bit better, whether by a healthy child, a garden patch, or a redeemed social condition; to know even one life has breathed easier because you have lived. This is to have succeeded."
~ Ralph Waldo Emerson

"If you carefully consider what you want to be said of you at your funeral . . . there you will find your definition of success."
~ Steven Covey

"Progress is my one-word definition of happiness. If you can have progress in your career, finances, family, spirituality, and your love life, no matter where you start, you will always be happy."
~ Sam Dogen (Financial Samurai founder)

"Each of us has two distinct choices to make about what we will do with our lives. The first choice we can make is to be less than we have the capacity to be. To earn less. To have less. To read less and think less. To try less and discipline ourselves less. These are the choices that lead to an empty life. These are the choices that, once made, lead to a life of constant apprehension instead of a life of wondrous anticipation. The second choice? To do it all! To become all that we can possibly be. To read every book that we possibly can. To earn as much as we possibly can. To give and share as much as we possibly can. To strive and produce and accomplish as much as we possibly can."
~ Jim Rohn

What is Your Purpose in Life?

At some point in our life, we will ask ourselves questions:

"Why am I here?"
"What is the purpose of life?"
 "Is there more?"
"What happens to us after we die?"
"Why should I care or strive?"

You're not alone. These questions are common, and I ask myself these questions. On my journey this far, in regard to what my purpose in life should be, I've found that the answers include:

• The purpose of life is to live a life of purpose.
• To leave the world a better place than I found it.
• To leave this world having lived an exhilarating life.
• To make continual progress towards worthy goals.

The problem is, to live your life without a purpose, feels the same as chartering a boat without a rudder, not knowing where you'll end up. You could get lucky and end up somewhere fantastic, but likely you'll end up running into shore somewhere mediocre, after having drifted aimlessly at sea for much of your journey.

The alternative to living your life without purpose is to live a life that you can live to the fullest, achieving purposeful goals that you never thought were possible, and live a life that can be summarized by the statement, "**WOW, what a life!**"

In the 1980s, I discovered the teachings of someone considered to be America's foremost business philosopher, who has inspired me, more in life than any other person, to think about my purpose in life. I had the privilege of meeting him in the late 1990s, at a success conference he was speaking at in Toronto. Throughout this book, you'll see some of my favourite quotes from Jim, who passed away in 2009, from which there are literally hundreds to choose from. Below is a personal favourite, which pertains to striving to be our best.

Why 100 Goals?

There is magic in numbers. Think about the special numbers that are celebrated in life. The most special are . . .

- Your 10th, 20th, 30th, 40th, 50th . . . 100th birthdays.
- Top 100 Places to See before you Die
- Billboard Hot 100
- The 100 most influential people in history

In fact, when you google search *Top 100*, there are over 1 billion hits. Clearly, people are obsessed with the number, *one hundred*. So am I. As I prepared for my 30th birthday, I was inspired to write out a list of 100 lifetime goals. Why 100? Because 10 is too few, and 1,000 is too many. *One hundred* felt like the perfect number. It is a big enough number that when you break it down into subcategories, it splits nicely into 10 categories of 10 sub goals. You'll notice that there are 10 subcategories of goals, with 10 sub goals, written about in this book. For the same reason as the number 100, there is the same magic with the number ten. There are even more Top 10 lists. When designing your life, consider 100 as your perfect number of goals to help start designing your life.

The 80/20 Rule and Your Top 20!

There is a famous rule, known as the Pareto principle, which says that 80% of the results of any activity are desired from just 20% of the effort. It is also known as the law of the vital few. Said in other ways:

- 80% of the effects come from 20% of the causes
- 80% of the sales come from 20% of the clients
- 20% of earners pay 80% of the taxes
- 20% of fitness exercise has 80% of the impact on your fitness
- 20% of people in an organization drive 80% of the results
- Etc.

In the context of this book, my challenge to you is to pick the top 20 (20%) of these 100 goals, which you believe will have the top 80% impact in your life. Don't stress over feeling that you need to do all 100 of these goals. Out of this list of

100 goals, there are likely 20 goals that will be the most relatable to you and have the potential to impact you the greatest (i.e. 80%).

Bucket List versus Goals?

This book is about well-designed goals to live your best life. A bucket list refers to the list of things that you want to do before you die, and it is a great thing to write for yourself. It was made popular by the 2007, American comedy-drama film, directed by Rob Reiner, called *The Bucket List*.

Examples of bucket list items include:

- Hang Gliding
- Riding in a hot air balloon
- Swimming with dolphins
- Horseback riding on the beach
- Standing under a waterfall
- Meeting a famous person
- Bicycling across the Golden Gate Bridge
- Seeing a Las Vegas show
- Setting a Guinness Book world record
- Flying in a private jet
- Taking a cooking class
- Learning another language
- Going deep sea fishing
- Flying in a helicopter
- Climbing a mountain

There are excellent websites about people who have been inspired to list 1,000 bucket list goals for their life and are going about achieving them. It is a very exciting and inspiring way to live your life.

The challenge with some bucket lists, however, is that the items that end up on many people's bucket lists are items that are more adventure, travel, and thrill-based—they omit the more important things in your life, as represented in the 10 Goal Areas of this book. The traditional *Bucket List* is to be included within the sections for Adventure Goals and Travel Goals. By all means, call these your bucket list goals.

A Life of WOW!

What would a life of WOW look like to you?   What does it take for you to say WOW when you are talking to another person and hear them explain some experience they've had?   What would it take to impress your very own self, where you would say, "WOW, I can't believe I just did that?"   Let me help paint the picture of what a life of WOW might look like:

- Incredible health, energy, and vitality
- Living to 100 years old (or older), and doing things that people half your age are still doing
- Traveling the world to exotic locations and experiencing different life cultures
- Money is not an obstacle in your life to living the life you've designed
- Close relationship with your spouse
- Nurturing relationships with your children
- A fulfilling career as an employee or business owner
- Having strong morals and values that you live by
- Living in your custom-designed dream house
- Owning a cottage or vacation retreat on a lake or in the woods
- Driving your dream car
- Helping others less fortunate than yourself
- And more . . .

The good news is that you are designing your life, and no two lives are the same. Your dream life will be entirely different to that of everyone else you know.   We are also starting from different places in our lives.   Some of us are fortunate to have been born to families in countries that already have a high level of prosperity. For those of you that are not, some of these goals will seem like an impossibility. For others, you may already have been living the dream life that countless others would die for.   The main point of this book is to inspire you to design a life, instead of just letting your life happen.   And while you're designing your life, why not design a life of WOW?   One of my very favourite quotes is by Bill McKenna . . .

"Life is not a journey to the grave with the intention of arriving safely in a pretty and well-preserved body, but rather to skid in sideways, thoroughly used up, totally worn out, and loudly proclaiming: WOW, what a ride!"

Living with No Regrets

The main concept of this book is to design your life so well that you end up at the end of your life with no regrets for not having lived your life a certain way. There are too many of us who live in our comfort zone.   If you live in your comfort zone your entire life, there is a high certainty that you will have some major regrets in your life.   There are so many people, when questioned during their last year of life about parting with any regrets, who respond with something like: I wish I . . .

• Risked more
• Loved more
• Worked less
• Let go of my grudges

In fact, nurses in hospitals or hospices are the ones that hear the regrets of the dying:

• I wish I'd had the courage to live the life I dreamed of, not the one that was expected of me.
• I wish I hadn't worked so many hours at work, at the expense of my family.
• I wish I had learned to express my feelings. Supressing feelings leads to poor relationships and regrets of what could have been, had you had the courage to make things right.
• I wish I had stayed in touch with my friends.
• I should have saved more money for my retirement.

Of these, the number one regret that people have on their death bed is that they did not pursue their dreams and goals. Don't be one of these people—start living a life that you design.

When your health and youth have faded, you'll reflect on what the important things in life are, and you will realize what is truly valuable . . . your friends and family.   That is why this book of 100 life goals has an entire section on setting friend and family goals.   There is no point in developing high net worth through working hard at your career or business, achieving all your goals but achieving a failing grade with your family.   The most important people are your friends and family.   Live your life so that they are there for you when you need them the most.

Knowing all of this, the purpose of this book is to inspire you to live your own unique, purposeful life.   Achieving just some of these 100 goals, or modifications to these 100 goals, is something you can do. You can go and live out your own life of WOW.   Live your life to avoid future regrets.   Said another way . . . **Live with No Regrets!**

WHY, WHEN, AND HOW TO SET GOALS

Written Goals?

Surveys reveal that people who write down their goals are 50% more likely to achieve success on many levels than people who don't. It is believed that less than 5 out of every 100 adults write down their goals on paper. The following are some interesting facts, statistics, and personal observations:

* More than 90% of New Year's goals fail by the end of January each year.
* A Harvard study suggests 83% of Americans don't have goals.
* Writing down of goals is a very powerful motivator.
* People are more likely to have business goals than goals for their own life.

Not many people talk about their goals in conversation (even myself, to this point). This needs to change.

One of the best quotes on why to set goals can be found on a YouTube video—Jim Rohn, Best Life Ever—at about the 49-minute mark, where he says . . .

> *"Goal Setting. The promise of the future is an awesome force to affect your life every day. Without a future well designed, we take hesitant steps. "*
> *– Jim Rohn*

Typical Goals vs. 100 Balanced Goals

When most people write goals, they focus on what I call the exciting goals, which are usually focused around travel, adventure, and lifestyle. These goals are very important and are the goals that will be motivating to achieve. Examples of these goals include:
* Climb Mount Everest

- Buy a high-end luxury or sports car
- Be a millionaire
- Travel the world
- Own a vacation property in Hawaii
- Safari in Africa

While it's entirely possible to achieve all of these goals, in doing so, it's possible that goal achievement will come at the expense of poor health, poor relationships, and generally a life that is focused too much in the areas that are money-driven. In writing this book and designing my own life, I've very carefully designed these goals to be *well-balanced* in all the key areas of life, to ensure that we end up living a balanced life, one that has you live with *no regrets*.   That is why these goals include goal areas, including:

- Personal Development
- Health and Fitness
- Family, Friends, and Social
- Giving Back, and Leaving a Legacy

That's not to say that your life needs to be balanced at all times. In fact, truly successful people live a life that is out of balance for periods of time, where they are focused on their important goals.   In my own life, there have been many times where I've been highly unbalanced for months at a time due to working excessive overtime in my career, or during a major house renovation. The problem becomes when you are out of balance for several years, or even an entire decade.   That's when relationships suffer, and your own health can deteriorate.   It's sometimes too late to regain these important areas once they are too far out of balance. Recognize the importance of having an overall balance in your life.

The Best Time to Set and Update Goals

In my younger years, by reading a good self-help book, or by listening to self-help audio tapes (cassette tapes now a thing of the past), I would be inspired to drive to a park during my lunch hour and ponder about goalsetting.   Think about the times when you've thought about goals and perhaps even written them down. The truth is that any time is a good time to be thinking about and writing down your goals, but there are times that have more meaning.   In my own life, I've gravitated towards writing my goals:

- While on vacation, sitting on a Lanai (veranda), or on the beach
- The week leading up to January 1st each year
- While sitting on a park bench, near a lake or ocean
- The month preceding a major decade birthday (i.e. my 20th, 30th, 40th and 50th birthdays, etc.)

In writing your own 100 life goals, the setting of good goals for your life does require some serious reflection, often enhanced by the passing of time and influenced by reflection that comes with the passing of a birthday, a calendar year, or the onset of a major decade birthday. My recommendation is that you start writing your goals NOW as you are inspired to do so, while reading this book, with the ultimate goal to write and commit to some of these goals before one of these next milestones:

- Your next birthday
- The end of this coming year

SMART Goals

Many people are familiar with the acronym, SMART, as it pertains to goal setting. All good sources about goals will reference this SMART acronym, for which goals are to be written as:

S – Specific
M – Measurable
A – Attainable
R – Relevant
T – Time bound

SPECIFIC

Be very specific about your goals. The following table illustrates a poorly written goal that is not specific, and a well written goal that is.

MEASUREABLE

Goals need to be measurable in terms of knowing whether or not you have achieved your goal or not. A goal that says, "I want to lose weight," is not measurable. A goal to lose a total of 25 lbs, is.

ATTAINABLE

Your *target* goals need to be attainable; your *outrageous* goals do not. Select target goals that any reasonable person (specifically you) would say, with dedicated effort and time, that they are attainable goals, given your current circumstances in life. If you currently have a 65% average in your senior year of high school, and you want to go to university to be a veterinarian or a doctor, it's not realistic to think you could attain that goal, due to the high entrance averages required for these programs, typically 90%+. As an outrageous goal, however, if you are passionate about this, definitely write it down.

RELEVANT

Goals need to be relevant to your life. To use the above example of being a doctor, if you currently have very little interest in the medical field and want to be a doctor because of the high-income potential, or because your parents want this for you, I would suggest to you that this goal is not relevant to who you are as a person. Choose goals that are relevant to you as a person and the life you want to live.

TIME BOUND

The *time* component of SMART goals is to be time specific, by saying when you will accomplish your goal. In setting life goals, the aspect of time achievement will likely be longer term than if you were establishing goals with a shorter horizon. It is best to establish goals that are a balance of short, medium, and long-term goals. If all your goals can be accomplished within the next year, then you are setting your goals too easy. If they will all take a *lifetime* to achieve, then they're too difficult. This guide will help you set goals that are a balance of goals you will accomplish within the next year, 5 years, 10 years, and within your lifetime.

Goals need a timeline to create a sense of urgency to get them done. With a firm due date that you committed to, your goals will drift. You don't need to worry about doing this for all 100 goals right now. Pick the most important top 10 or 20 that you will be serious about achieving, and give them firm due dates. Some of the goals you set will have a recurring time frame, meaning that you want to commit to achieving them annually or each decade.

Minimum, Target, and Outrageous (MTO) Goals

The very best goal setting system that I was fortunate to come across was the MTO system, developed by Raymond Aaron. His approach to goals is unique and one that guarantees success. Using the acronym, MTO, which stands for Minimum, Target, and Outrageous, goals are to be set at 3 levels to ensure you have an easily attainable goal (Minimum), a goal that is realistic for you (Target), and a goal that is a massive stretch goal (Outrageous).

MINIMUM

The concept of setting a *minimum* goal is to develop confidence, such that the minimum goal being set is easily attainable, something that you can be counted on to attain within the next week, month, or year. For the purpose of this book, because the focus is on longer-term goals and lifetime goals, the minimum goal is not focused on. I recommend you purchase Raymond Aaron's book, *Double Your Income Doing What You Love*, where this approach to setting minimum goals is explained fully. It is a powerful concept.

TARGET

Target goals are the focus of this book on developing 100 life goals. These are the goals that you will be targeting. They will be goals that are to meet the requirements of being a SMART goal. They are the goals that will be *stretch* goals, and they will require significant effort and planning to achieve. The important part is that you believe you will accomplish each of these goals within your life.

OUTRAGEOUS

There is a third category of goals, called *Outrageous:* the idea of setting goals that are so outrageous that you don't believe they are attainable, in direct contrast to the "A" in the SMART acronym, which stands for *Attainable*. This is particularly valuable within the framework for this book, *100 Life Goals*. This gives you permission to set goals that are far outside your comfort zone, which are truly inspiring to you but don't meet the requirements for attainability. The logic is that in setting outrageous goals, your subconscious mind will get to work in helping conspire to achieve your outrageous goals; and even though you believe they are unattainable at the time of writing the goal, it is possible, over time, that you will achieve some of your outrageous goals. As these 100 goals are lifetime goals, this is perfect. When I learned this system, it gave me the freedom to re-examine all my goals—and add an *outrageous* version of each of my 100 goals—to encourage me to strive further, well beyond my comfort zone, while giving me permission to not feel failure if they are not achieved. This is a liberating concept to know that you can set goals that are *shoot for the moon* type goals. An example from my own 100 goals is as follows:

Target Goal: Take a 100-kilometer bicycle ride.

Outrageous Goal: Ride my bicycle around Lake Ontario, the 14th largest lake in the world, with a shore length of 1,020 Km (634 miles).

For me, setting a target goal of riding a 100-Km bike ride will be a significant achievement, given that my longest bike ride to date has been approximately 10 Km. Setting an *outrageous* goal of riding around one of the largest lakes in my country of Canada—which will take approximately 10 days to accomplish—is beyond what seems attainable to me but is also something that with extreme commitment, could be accomplished within my lifetime.

I've taught this MTO approach for goal setting to my staff where I work, and have included this into our annual performance review process. At the time of writing this book, we are currently in the process of establishing approximately 15 SMART goals as part of our Strategic Goal Deployment (SGD) process, establishing minimum, target, and outrageous goals to accomplish, with a lead person assigned to each of the 15 goals.

ONE HUNDRED GOALS

Ten Essential Life Goal Areas

In designing your balanced life, one with no regrets, goals are to be written in 10 categories.

- Personal Development
- Health and Fitness
- Family and Friends
- Hobbies and Passions
- Financial
- Career
- Adventure
- Travel
- Lifestyle
- Leaving a Legacy

The above goal areas are listed in a rank order that, in my opinion, represent the priority in which they should be viewed within the context of your life.

Our success in life begins with our own commitment to personal development, which is the reason I've started with it. Next is your own personal health. Without good health, the rest of our goal accomplishment and life suffers. Next is family and friends. There is no point in being successful with your career and lifestyle goals without a strong foundation of family and friends. Then there are your hobbies and passions, which are the things you truly love doing. These need to be a priority in your life, otherwise they will fall victim to your career, which is the next important goal area.

The challenge with listing these goals in a ranked sequence like this, is that this is just my personal opinion, and you may have a different view. That's okay. The most important thing is that you are setting and achieving balanced goals across this list of 10 goal areas.

At the end of your life, in your last 5–10 years, it's highly likely that the importance of these goal areas will completely change to something like:

- Family and Friends
- Health and Fitness
- Leaving a Legacy
- Hobbies and Passions
- Lifestyle
- Financial
- Adventure
- Travel
- Career
- Personal Development

When you are in in your final days, the most important questions will be, *"Who do I love?"* and, *"Who loves me?"* This is critically important to understand *now*, so that you live your life keeping these important family and friend relationships alive. Your health is also of critical importance, as you don't want to be saying to yourself, *"I wish I would have taken better care of my health,"* after it's too late to do something about it.

Most of the goal setting self-help books and programs I listened to in my early days seemed to focus on the exciting goals—the more traditional goals—related to lifestyle, travel, and adventure goals. These are the goals that are easier to write and get excited about. These goals are important to living a good life too. They are often the goals that provide the *why*. Why do I need to strive and improve and grow? Why do I need to develop myself and have a great career? Besides providing for my family, it's to live the good life, to travel the world, to live in a nice house, and to not have to worry about money constantly.

The 100 Life Goals are goals that I've modified from my original list of 100 goals, created at the age of 30, to have more universal appeal to the majority of people living in the developed world. While they are goals that I think you will find important, you may find some of them to be completely irrelevant for you. If you do, there is no problem in changing any of them, or all of them. My main hope is that they give you ideas and inspire you to create your own list of *100 Life Goals*.

Take the time to design these goals that inspire you to live fully.

"Goals. There's no telling what you can do when you get inspired by them. There's no telling what you can do when you believe in them. There's no telling what will happen when you act upon them." ~ Jim Rohn

As I mentioned earlier, I learned an amazing affirmation while attending a Masterkey seminar, hosted by my Karate Sensei, in the late 1980s. The affirmation, "I am happy, healthy, wealthy, and wise," has been a central and major influence in my life. Another way to segregate the 10 goal areas written in this book, instead of numbering them 1 through 10, would be to categorize them into this great affirmation.

Happy Goals	Healthy Goals	Wealthy Goals	Wise Goals
3) Family and Friends	2) Health and Fitness	5) Financial	1) Personal Development
4) Hobbies and Passions		6) Career	10) Leaving a Legacy
7) Adventure			
8) Travel			
9) Lifestyle			

I feel so strongly about this affirmation that more than 20 years ago, I developed a system for filing my goals into these categories, and gave each category a color:

- Blue for Happy – blue sky, blue water, calmness
- Red for Healthy – red blood, red tomatoes, red apples
- Green for Wealthy – the color of money
- Grey for Wise – wise older people (and their grey hair)

My wife and I actually chose to have our four heritage homes painted these 4 colors. Check out www.GablesOnThePark.com to see how it turned out.

Writing Your Goals

Each of the upcoming *100 Life Goals* is discussed in a consistent guide format, written to inspire you to write either the same goal or spawn an idea for a similar goal that is more uniquely relevant to your own life. I have given examples of my own goals, as I believe it is powerful to help your goal development process by reading about what is important in another person's life. Each of the 100 goals follows the same layout:

Goal # and Title Description – This is one of the 100 goals, written in a short form *summary* method.

Reason for this Goal – Explanation on why this goal is important.

Further thoughts about this Goal – Personal thoughts and ideas about this goal.

Suggested Target Goal(s) – Either a restatement of the Goal from item # 1 above, or a more specific goal, or goal suggestions for you to consider for your own life.

Outrageous Goal – This is a sample of what should be viewed as highly desirable but likely an impossible goal based on your current place in life. But just thinking about it as a possibility inspires you (or possibly scares you . . . in a good way).

Your Target Goal (YTG) – This is a place for you to write your own goal. Don't worry about writing in this book; it is meant to be a useful working guide that you can refer to often. If you change it later, just cross it out and write in the margins. Your Outrageous Goal – Go ahead; write your own outrageous goal. Don't worry that you ever have to achieve it! But who knows, you just might!

Adapt what you find as useful, and reject what isn't; and add goals that resonate with who you are or want to be.

PERSONAL DEVELOPMENT GOALS

While it may seem odd to set goals related to personal development, this will be the foundation for you in accomplishing these 100 life goals. From a long-term perspective, there is no point in setting easy goals. Since the goals will be challenging to accomplish, it stands to reason that you will need to develop yourself as a person in order to accomplish them. The following 10 goals, under this category of *Personal Development Goals,* are designed to help you achieve all of the balance of your 100 goals. They will also help you grow as a person and become the person you are capable of becoming. Don't take these goals lightly. They are critically important to designing and living the life of your dreams—living your life and being able to say, "Wow, I did that!"

My 10 goals in this area are as follows:

- Read (study) the field of Self-Help
- Define your core values
- Attend personal development seminars
- Develop a daily Power Hour
- Find a mentor
- Learn continuously
- Develop your Positive Attitude
- Develop your communication skill
- Write your life purpose
- Discover your spirituality

Adopt, modify, or change these 10 goals to make them your own.

"You will be the same person in five years as you are today, except for the people you meet and the books you read." – Charlie Tremendous Jones

Goal # 1 – Read (study) Self-Help

Reason for this Goal: The self-help field is made up of hundreds of successful people in all areas of life, who have written books and recorded audio, providing information and tips on why and how to achieve all the possible goals you wish to achieve in your life. This is the information that in a perfect world, would be taught to you within the school system. Reading is a fundamental strategy to continue to learn throughout your life; and why not read about strategies on how to live a better life?

Most people never read another non-fiction book after they graduate from school. Don't let that be you. It is said that there are really only two things that change people . . . the books that you read and the people that you meet. Reading books by people who understand what it takes to be successful, and who have already led amazing lives, are invaluable on your success journey. What books should you read? Below is a list of suggested book topics, and some book titles, which I've personally read:

- The Magic of Thinking Big
- Younger Next Year
- Rich Dad Poor Dad
- The One Minute Millionaire
- Double Your Income Doing What You Love (by Raymond Aaron)
- Think and Grow Rich (by Napoleon Hill)
- The Blue Zones (a book about longevity)
- The Happiness Equation
- The Millionaire Next Door
- Body for Life

By reading a great book by an influential person, you can actually get into the mind of that great person and learn all about what they were thinking, and their advice for you. Some powerful advice that Robin Sharma's dad (the father of one of the great, living, self-help gurus) told him was, *"Cut back on your rent, or cut back on what you spend on food, but never worry about investing money in a good book."* It just takes one idea discovered in a single book to completely change your life. Try and devote at least 20 minutes a day to reading. An hour is even better. If you truly want to be a leader and live a goal inspired life, you need to make time to read. Some of the busiest and most successful people in the world take time to read 1 hour a day, including Warren Buffet, Bill Gates, and even Barrack Obama, while he was serving as President of the USA.

Make it your mission to find the authors and speakers who will help accelerate your goal attainment and improve your life. Go to any library or book store, and you should find a self-help section.

A list of some of the **legends** in the Personal Development field, as rated by www.success.com, including their most recognized work, include:

- Dale Carnegie (1888–1955) – How to Win Friends and Influence People
- George Clason (1874–1957) – *The Richest Man in Babylon*
- Stephen Covey (1932–2012) – The 7 Habits of Highly Effective People
- Viktor Frankl (1905–1997) – *Man's Search for Meaning*
- Napoleon Hill (1883–1970) – *Think and Grow Rich*
- Charlie "Tremendous" Jones (1927–2008) – *Life is Tremendous*
- Og Mandino (1923–1996) – The Greatest Salesman in the World
- Orison Swett Marden (1850–1924) – Founder of *Success* magazine
- Earl Nightingale (1921–1989) – *The Strangest Secret*, and *Lead the Field*
- Norman Vincent Peale (1898–1993) – *The Power of Positive Thinking*
- Jim Rohn (1930–2009) – The Art of Exceptional Living
- W. Clement Stone (1902–2002) – Success Through a Positive Mental Attitude
- Zig Ziglar (1926–2012) – *See You at the Top*

The above legends have all passed, but they have inspired many of the current leaders in the field of personal development. The following includes a list of people as rated by *Success* magazine, based on the number of people their work positively influenced in 2014, listed in alphabetical order:

- Martha Beck – Finding Your Own North Star
- Ken Blanchard – The One Minute Manager, and Refire! Don't Retire
- Les Brown – It's Not Over Until You Win
- Brendon Burchard – The Motivation Manifesto
- Jack Canfield – Chicken Soup for the Soul series, and The Power of Focus
- Deepak Chopra – The 7 Spiritual Laws of Success
- Henry Cloud – *Boundaries* series
- Wayne Dyer – Your Erroneous Zones, and The Power of Intention

- Tim Ferriss – The 4-Hour Workweek
- Seth Godin – Linchpin; Tribes; and The Dip
- Steve Harvey – Act Like a Lady, Think Like a Man
- Arianna Huffington – On Becoming Fearless . . . in Love, Work, Life
- T.D. Jakes – Instinct: The Power to Unleash Your Inborn Drive
- Robert Kiyosaki – *Rich Dad, Poor Dad* series
- John Maxwell – The 21 Irrefutable Laws of Leadership
- Suze Orman – *The Suze Orman Show* (financial education)
- Joel Osteen – Your Best Life Now, and Become a Better You
- Mehmet Oz (Dr. Oz) – *YOU: The Owner's Manual* (Health Expert)
- Dave Ramsey – The Total Money Makeover
- Tony Robbins – Awaken the Giant Within, and Unlimited Power
- Robin Roberts – From the Heart: Seven Rules to Live By
- Sheryl Sandberg – Lean In: Women, Work, and the Will to Lead
- Robin Sharma – The Monk Who Sold His Ferrari
- Brian Tracy – Eat That Frog! and The Psychology of Achievement
- Oprah Winfrey – The Oprah Winfrey Show

In addition to this, there are hundreds of autobiographies of famous, living (and deceased) people who have written their life stories, from which you can learn immensely. These can be even more inspiring.

I have read many of these books. It is my conviction that for those of us that want for a better life, there is no better way to get inspired than by reading and listening to programs by these types of authors and speakers, and to the thousands of people that they have inspired to lead better lives as a result.

You can literally find books and programs to help target every one of these 100 goals, should you want or need help in what to do next.

Did you know that more than 80% of people have not bought a book in the past year, or that more than 70% have not in the past 5 years? More than 40% of college graduates never read another book in their lifetime. The percentages are even higher for non-fiction books. With these kinds of statistics, you can see how easy it would be to set yourself apart from the average person just by reading books, especially of the self-help type.

If you really don't like reading books, listening to pod casts are an excellent way to learn the same information.

Suggested Target Goal: Read 10 self-help books.

Outrageous Goal: Read 100+ self-help and non-fiction books (Never stop reading.).

Your Goals:

Your Target Goal (YTG): _____

Your Outrageous Goal: _____

Timeline to complete YTG: [ ] This Year [ ] 3 Years [ ] 10 Years [ ] Lifetime

"If you read only one book per month, that will put you into the top 1% of income earners in our society. But if you read one book per week, 50 books per year, that will make you one of the best educated, smartest, most capable and highest paid people in your field. Regular reading will transform your life completely." – Brian Tracy

Goal # 2 – Define Your Core Values

Reason for this Goal: Knowing and being true to your core values will help you with all the decisions in your life. They will act as your *internal compass* and serve as a lens through which you view the world. They will help determine how you will be remembered and what kind of legacy you will leave. You will be happiest when you are living in harmony with your core values, once you are intentional about adhering to them.

Values are your personal attributes that you stand for, no matter what. What do you put above all else in terms of defining who you are? There are many values you can choose as your core values. Some examples, listed in alphabetical order, include:

- Achievement, Adventure, Action, Ambitious
- Balance
- Calm, Candid, Caring, Charity, Collaboration, Commitment, Communication, Compassion, Confidence, Contribution, Courage, Creativity, Compassion, Curiosity, Customer Service
- Dedication, Dependability, Determination, Disciplined, Doer, Driven
- Education, Effective, Efficient, Empathetic, Empowered, Encouragement, Energetic, Engagement, Enthusiasm, Entrepreneurship, Ethical, Excellence
- Faith, Family, Famous, Fearlessness, Friendly, Fun
- Generosity, Giving, Goodness, Grateful, Gratitude, Growth
- Happiness, Hard work, Health, Honesty, Honor, Humble, Humour
- Impact, Independence, Innovation, Integrity, Intelligence
- Joyful
- Kindness, Knowledge
- Leadership, Learning, Legacy, Listening, Love, Loyalty
- Mastery, Meaning, Meticulous, Modesty, Motivation
- Neatness, Noble
- Openness, Opportunity, Optimism
- Passion, Patient, Patriotism, Peace, People, Perseverance, Persistence, Personal Development, Personal Growth, Philanthropy, Playfulness, Positivity, Politeness, Progress, Prosperity
- Quality
- Realistic, Recreation, Reflection, Reliability, Resilience, Resourceful, Respect, Responsible

- Sacrifice, Self-Awareness, Self-Control, Selfless, Sense of Humour, Service, Sincerity, Spirituality, Strength, Success
- Team work, Togetherness, Tolerance, Toughness, Transparency, Trust, Truth
- Unique, Useful
- Valor, Virtuous, Vision, Vitality
- Wisdom, Wonder
- Yes-minded, Youthful
- Zen

Suggested Target Goal: List your Core Values and live by them.

Outrageous Goal: Be true to your Core Values 100% of the time.

You should choose between 3 and 7 Core Values. Some Core Values of famous people:

- Oprah Winfrey: Courage, Perseverance, Generosity, Progress, Sincerity
- Henry Ford: Goodness, Sincerity, Generosity, Progress, Perseverance

My core values are:

- Integrity
- Optimism
- Courage
- Encouragement
- Knowledge

Of all the values listed, the most important is Integrity. Raymond Aaron says, in one of his one-minute monthly mentor videos, that if you have integrity, nothing else matters. Warren Buffet says that Integrity is the only thing that matters when hiring someone.

Choose your core values this year, and update them once a year as you get better insights into who you are and who you want to be. When you have a tough decision to make, think about your core values, and this will make your decision easier to make.

Your Goals:

Your Target Goal (YTG) (YTG): _____

Your Outrageous Goal: _____

Timeline to complete YTG: [ ] This Year [ ] 3 Years [ ] 10 Years [ ] Lifetime

Goal # 3 – Attend Personal Development Seminars

Reason for this Goal: Attending conferences or workshops led by success-oriented speakers is a great way to keep inspired and motivated to achieve your goals. Your life will be lifted and energized after attending a personal development seminar. Attending one with your partner is a great strategy for staying connected and together as you develop your life strategies.

Writing this goal is straight forward. You just need to decide that this is important, and write your goal to attend at least one seminar per year.

Suggested Target Goal: Attend at least one success workshop annually.

Outrageous Goal: Be a teacher at a major success conference.

Over the years, I have attended workshops such as:

- Improve Your Life Seminar
- Master Key Seminar
- Real Estate Wealth Expo, with guest speaker, Tony Robbins
- Self-help seminars, with guest speakers, including Jim Rohn, Robin Sharma, and Brian Tracy
- Raymond Aaron's Monthly Mentor, 2-day workshop

There are numerous events that are held every year in cities around the world, which you can attend. Find something that you connect with, and sign up. Consider the cost to attend as an investment in your future. Invest in yourself as much as you can. Anything you invest in yourself, you will get back tenfold.

Your Goals:

Your Target Goal (YTG): _____

Your Outrageous Goal: _____

Timeline to complete YTG: [ ] This Year [ ] 3 Years [ ] 10 Years [ ] Lifetime

Goal # 4 – Develop a "Power Hour"

Reason for this Goal: The way you spend the first hour of each day is the most important hour of the day. Most, if not all, successful people have developed morning rituals before they get on to their daily business. Many successful people practice a 5am wake-up, and acknowledge this practice as key to their success.

Establish a goal to develop your own power hour filled with things that align best with you. Examples of actions that could comprise your Power Hour include:

- Exercise
- Writing
- Goal planning
- Meditation
- Tai Chi or Yoga
- Journaling
- Doing nothing and thinking nothing

My power hour begins at 5am, which I do 5 days/week, vacation time excluded. It includes 30 minutes of exercise, 10 minutes of journaling, and 10 minutes of either writing, goal planning, or contemplating thinking.

Ask people what they do in the morning and if they have their own version of a power hour. It reveals a lot about a person.

Suggested Target Goal: Develop the habit of a Power Hour.

Outrageous Goal: Continue the Power Habit, 5 days/week, for life.

Your Goals:

Your Target Goal (YTG): _____

Your Outrageous Goal: _____

Timeline to complete YTG: [ ] This Year [ ] 3 Years [ ] 10 Years [ ] Lifetime

Goal # 5 – Find a Mentor

Reason for this Goal: Finding a mentor who is someone you would like to learn from or be like can help you enormously in becoming the person you want to be, much quicker than on your own.

Besides my parents—parents start off as your most important mentors—my Karate Sensei was my first and most influential mentor. I then found mentorship through listening to self-help experts like Brian Tracy, Les Brown, and my personal favourite, Jim Rohn. I would listen to these mentors while driving my car and during my lunch hours, through most of my twenties. I then found my mentor at a local Toastmasters club while learning to improve and develop my public speaking.

I have been fortunate to have good mentors in my life, although I did not formally recognize that's what they were until later in life. Raymond Aaron has multiple mentors for each of the key areas in his life. I think that is a great idea and plan to someday do the same thing. Why not have a specific mentor for each of these 10 goal areas? At least, have someone you can look up to in these areas, even if you can't call them your mentor.

The most successful people who have achieved greatness all have mentors; why not you? The easiest way to find a mentor is to go to the self-help section of your local book store, and find an author whom you connect with through their books and teachings. You can also look to the people you know, approach one of them whom you believe in, and ask them if they'd be interested in mentoring you. Most people, regardless of their level of success, would be flattered as most never get asked. There are also people with professions, such as a Life Coach, who can mentor you on what you need to do. Potential areas for which you need mentors include all the core areas for goals that you'll read about in this book—a business mentor, a health or fitness mentor, a financial mentor—some of the most successful people have multiple mentors and coaches . . . for all the important areas in their life.

You could agree to meet monthly or quarterly, where you will each discuss the areas of your life that you are working on, including specific goals and timelines. Knowing that you will be meeting to discuss your progress will give you a heightened level of awareness and accountability towards your goals, in addition to valuable feedback from your group.

Suggested Target Goal: Find a mentor/coach.

Outrageous Goal: Meet your mentor(s) monthly for the rest of your life.

Your Goals:

Your Target Goal (YTG): _____

Your Outrageous Goal: _____

Timeline to complete YTG: [ ] This Year [ ] 3 Years [ ] 10 Years [ ] Lifetime

Goal # 6 – Learn Continuously

Reason for this Goal: Learning for the mind is equivalent to exercise for the body. New information acquired through reading books and talking to people will change your life. Make it your mission to learn as much as you can about as much as you can. Ask questions without the fear of appearing stupid. This is one of the sad realities; some of us fear asking questions, fearing how we will be perceived.

One of the key areas that requires a continual focus to keep up the learning curve is technology, as well as a general curiosity of learning about the world:

• Apple products (iPhone, iMac computer, etc.)
• Artificial Intelligence (AI)
• Automobile technology (our vehicle's computer system)
• Environmental change
• Entrepreneurship
• Health and wellness
• History of the world
• Robotic products (coming soon)
• Solar power
• The internet of things
• And so much more . . .

One of the greatest websites I feel fortunate to have been introduced to, is a website called www.**Waitbuywhy.com.** The founder of this site does a *deep dive* into a wide variety of topics that most people only have a basic concept of, in an easy to understand format, complete with simple illustrations.

Suggested Target Goal: List and learn about the key technologies that are part of my life.

My Outrageous Goal: Learn about one new topic each day.

This approach to learning, and making learning a focus through the establishment of monthly learning goals, is an important and exciting goal area. The best way to learn is by talking to people and reading books.

Just recently, I was speaking to a wise, 85-year-old man, named Peter, in a local grocery store. During our 15-minute conversation, he recommended I read the book, *A Short History of Nearly Everything,* written by Bill Bryson, and have my children read this also, as a life changing book. I can't wait!

Your Goals:

Your Target Goal (YTG): _____

Your Outrageous Goal: _____

Timeline to complete YTG: [ ] This Year [ ] 3 Years [ ] 10 Years [ ] Lifetime

"The only thing worse than not reading a book in the last ninety days is not reading a book in the last ninety days and thinking that it doesn't matter." – Jim Rohn

Goal # 7 – Develop Your Positive Attitude (Habit)

Reason for this Goal: Your attitude will ultimately determine your success in your life and contribute to your overall level of happiness.   There are people who have predominantly positive attitudes and those that have predominantly negative attitudes.   The analogy of whether you think of your glass as *half-empty* or *half-full* is a good one.   It is easy to let your attitude slide from positive to negative, since much of the news we are exposed to daily is negative.   The people that you enjoy being around the most are the people that have predominantly positive attitudes. The best way to help improve your attitude is to change the *self-talk* that is happening in your thoughts every day, by introducing positive affirmations that you repeat to yourself daily.   A positive affirmation, which I learned over 30 years ago and still repeat almost daily, is, "I am happy, healthy, wealthy and wise." There are numerous other examples of positive affirmations that you can use, such as . . .

* I have the ability to accomplish any task I set my mind to.
* I am connected to an unlimited source of abundance.
* I can accomplish anything I set my mind to.

Search the web for examples of positive affirmations you can introduce into your life.   Select a few that align with you the best, and start saying them to yourself every day.

Suggested Target Goal: Develop 3 positive affirmations and repeat daily.

Outrageous Goal: Be the most positive person of anyone you know.

Listen carefully to your inner voice to ensure you are thinking predominantly positive thoughts. This is crucial to being able to live out these 100 goals.

One of the things I'm currently struggling with is my desire to keep up with the news. The challenge is that the news is predominantly negative and really distorts the amount of negative news in the world, versus all the positive news that is of less interest to follow and doesn't sell newspapers. While I believe it is important to know what is going in the world, it's important to not let that influence your desire and need for a predominantly positive attitude.

Another great approach to life, I recently read about, is to decide whether you are an energy giver or an energy taker. Think about it in terms of when you are interacting with other people—are you leaving them with more positive energy, or less, once you leave their presence? I've decided that I want to be an energy giver, and to be one of the most positive people I know.

"The longer I live, the more I realize the impact of attitude on life. Attitude, to me, is more important than facts. It is more important than the past, the education, the money, than circumstances, than failure, than successes, than what other people think or say or do. It is more important than appearance, giftedness or skill. It will make or break a company... a church... a home. The remarkable thing is we have a choice everyday regarding the attitude we will embrace for that day. We cannot change our past... we cannot change the fact that people will act in a certain way. We cannot change the inevitable. The only thing we can do is play on the one string we have, and that is our attitude. I am convinced that life is 10% what happens to me and 90% of how I react to it. And so, it is with you... we are in charge of our Attitudes."
– Charles R. Swindoll

Your Goals:

Your Target Goal (YTG): _____

Your Outrageous Goal: _____

Timeline to complete YTG: [ ] This Year [ ] 3 Years [ ] 10 Years [ ] Lifetime

Goal # 8 – Develop Your Communication Skill

Reason for this Goal: Good communication skill is essential for life, whether it's for good relationships with our friends and family, or for developing within our chosen career. If your communication skills, such as talking, speaking, listening, and writing, are poor, they may limit your success in some key areas. There are hundreds of books and courses available to read and attend that will help you in these areas. Decide which of these skills are in areas you need to improve on, and which will help you the most, and develop a plan. Dale Carnegie, a legendary person in the self-help field, developed a program called *The Dale Carnegie Course in Effective Speaking and Human Relations*. It is a learn-by-doing based program. It was founded in 1912, and is represented in over 90 countries. More than 8 million people have completed Dale Carnegie Training.

Of all the communication skills, many successful people, at some point in their life or career, will need to speak publicly. One of the biggest fears people have, sometimes more than dying, is the fear of public speaking. If you can overcome this fear and make it a strength (or, at a minimum, something you can do with a reasonable comfort level), you will advance your life. You will get promoted faster. You will be able to inspire others to action. Examples of times in which you will be called on to speak in public include . . .

- At a wedding (as a bride, groom, best man, or maid of honor)
- As you develop your career and are called upon to address others
- Toasting others on their special milestone birthdays or anniversaries
- As a guest speaker at a special event

As my daughter pointed out to me while writing this book, not everyone is going to want to embrace public speaking as something they want to aspire towards. Choose one of the important communication skills to work on instead, and realize that communicating well is a key life skill. The areas to work on include:

- Listening
- Conversation
- Reading
- Writing
- Speaking
- Storytelling

One of the best ways to develop your communication skills and become comfortable—and even good—with public speaking, is to join your local Toastmasters chapter. There are chapters in most cities throughout the world. I joined Toastmasters after accepting an invitation to speak about my career in the Bids and Proposals field. It is a positive and nurturing environment, with people that help you learn and develop. The cost is reasonable, and the classes are held weekly.

Some people are gifted communicators, but others, like myself, need to constantly work at it.

Suggested Target Goal: Join Toastmasters and obtain the 1st level of mastery.

Outrageous Goal: Become the best communicator in your company or chosen career.

Your Goals:

Your Target Goal (YTG): _____

Your Outrageous Goal: _____

Timeline to complete YTG: [ ] This Year [ ] 3 Years [ ] 10 Years [ ] Lifetime

Goal # 9 – Write Your Life Purpose

Reason for this Goal: Having a Life Mission will give your life more purpose. It will give more meaning to everything you do; and it will help guide your key decisions in life.

Developing your life purpose or mission statement will come into focus once you ask yourself some key questions:

- How do I want to be remembered at my funeral (What would I like people to be saying about me?)?
- What are the top 3 most important things in my life, to which I must devote most of my time and energy?
- Who do I really want to be?

The challenge is that finding your life mission is not something easy—and many people never do. The author, Cal Newport, suggests that discovering your life mission is something that can only be accomplished once you've developed your career to a point where your own unique skills and passions have revealed themselves. Until that happens, these types of questions are best contemplated when you have some alone time in nature—either in a park or forest, or at the lake or ocean.

Suggested Target Goal: To figure out and write your life purpose.

Outrageous Goal: To accomplish all 100 of these outrageous goals.

My life purpose, which has evolved, been written and re-written several times, and has been inspired by the teachings of Raymond Aaron, is:

- To be a good husband and father.
- To live and teach a goal-inspired life around *100 Life Goals*.
- To promote real estate investing as a key wealth building strategy.

Your Target Goal (YTG): _____

Your Outrageous Goal: _____

Timeline to complete YTG: [ ] This Year [ ] 3 Years [ ] 10 Years [ ] Lifetime

Goal # 10 – Discover Your Spirituality

Reason for this Goal: It is said that we all have a mind, a body, and a spirit. For many of us, it is tangible to understand one's mind and body, but the spirit is more allusive and the subject of many interpretations and beliefs. For some, a strong spirituality is the essence of life. For others, we're still working to understand the role of spirituality in our life.

Different people and cultures have spiritual beliefs that center around:

- An individual practice, and having a sense of peace and purpose
- Connection with a higher power (e.g., Universal Mind/Universalism)
- Life's greater purpose
- Meditation
- Metaphysics
- One of 19 major religious groupings in the world
- The law of attraction
- The meaning of life and connection with others
- Transcendentalism

It is important to note that there is no single, widely agreed definition of spirituality. But one thing is for sure, people that have a strong belief system around their spirituality are more grounded, and they have a strong foundation for who they are and what they believe in. If you have strong spirituality, that is fantastic, and it will serve you well in establishing your own goals. If you are still searching like me, use this goal to inspire you to keep searching until you find your own meaning.

Suggested Target Goal: Develop your own belief around spirituality.

Outrageous Goal: Have eternal faith with your spirituality to guide you through the rest of your life.

Your Target Goal (YTG): _____

Outrageous Goal: _____

Timeline to complete YTG: [ ] This Year [ ] 3 Years [ ] 10 Years [ ] Lifetime

HEALTH AND FITNESS GOALS

Out of all the 10 goal areas, achieving good health and fitness is one of the most important things we can hope to accomplish and maintain throughout our life. A healthy body and a healthy mind is the starting point for everything we do. Ask someone who is in poor health what they desire, and they will respond that getting back their good health is at the top of their list. It is my belief that we need to consciously focus on setting goals, work diligently every day to maximize our potential, and work to improve our health, such that we are in our optimum state each and every day.

My 10 goals in this important area are designed to help you get healthy and fit, and have some fun too:

- Eat healthy
- Maintain your ideal body weight
- Get aerobically fit
- Be strong - lift weights
- Develop a calm mind
- Learn how to prepare healthy meals
- Learn self defence
- Complete an endurance event
- Play a sport

Develop a long-life mindset. One of the primary ways to monitor how you are doing with your health is how you feel. While the main goal cited by young people for exercising is to look good, as we get older, the majority of us exercise for our health. While many of us focus on one type of exercise—such as running, spinning, or working out on a treadmill—we should be varying our exercise to get a cross section of training, which covers strength, stamina, and mobility. Being fit helps us fight the effects of aging and improves both our mental and physical health. The 10 goals recommended in this guide are designed to give you the balanced approach to achieving good health and fitness. Adopt, modify, or change these goals to make them your own.

Goal # 11 – Eat Healthy (Habit)

Reason for this Goal: To accomplish your *100 Life Goals*, you will need to have good health.   To feel good and happy, we need to be in good health.   Without good health, not much else matters.   One of the primary determinants of good health is what you put in your body.   There are other determinants of good health, like exercise and positive attitude, but what you eat is near the top of the list. What you eat also effects your moods.   You can easily get fooled into thinking that what you eat is not important, especially when you eat junk food and it doesn't seem to impact your health.   The impacts of poor eating will eventually catch up with you.   Most of us, by now, know what eating healthy entails, although there is so much conflicting information.   This is my list:

- Minimize or eliminate *junk* and processed foods . . . foods with white powders: processed sugar, excessive salt, white flour.
- Eat fruit, nuts, vegetables, and salad (raw, as much as possible).
- Eat reasonable portions, and only when your body is hungry (very important to long life).
- Drink plenty of water.
- Buy a blender or juicing machine, and use it daily.
- If you eat meat, choose poultry, fish, or seafood. Minimize red meat.
- Stop eating, 2 hours before bedtime.

I have another principle I've tried to teach my children: to "eat an apple a day;" however, it's not necessarily a proven health principle, but it is one I believe in. If you are like most people, you will go through life in phases, where you follow a good, eat-healthy regiment but then fall out.   The important thing is that you get back on track.

Suggested Target Goal: Develop your list of health principles and stick to it.

Outrageous Goal: Totally eliminate processed food from your diet.

Your Target Goal (YTG): _____

Your Outrageous Goal: _____

Timeline to complete YTG: [ ] This Year [ ] 3 Years [ ] 10 Years [ ] Lifetime

Goal # 12 – Maintain Your Ideal Body Weight

Reason for this Goal: A healthy body can take many forms and appearances. Most people would agree that maintaining your ideal body weight not only ensures you look and feel good, it also is indicative that you are not overconsuming junk food or too much food in general. The authors of the book, *Blue Zones*, researched groups, around the world, that have the longest life spans, and they found that people who ate small portions and maintained an ideal body weight were much more likely to live longer and healthier. Low caloric intake and *eating less* is viewed to be one of the best and scientifically proven ways to live longer and healthier.

Most of us already know, if asked what their ideal body weight should be. If you are fortunate, you are already at your ideal body weight. If you're not, or aren't sure what your ideal body weight should be, see your doctor. As you get older, it seems to get harder and harder to maintain your ideal body weight. But with a commitment to the 10 health goals suggested here, you will be on the right path to achieving your ideal body weight. The results will speak for themselves. One of the biggest benefits is that you will wake up and feel good about yourself each day.

Suggested Target Goal: Reach and maintain your ideal body weight for 1 year.

Outrageous Goal: Maintain your ideal body weight for life.

I've been fortunate to maintain my weight within 15 lbs of what I weighed 25 years ago when I was married.   It can be a struggle with the *battle of the bulge,* in spite of a good exercise program and reasonable health habits. The focus on this goal is important for your long-term health.

Your Goals:

Your Target Goal (YTG): _____

Your Outrageous Goal: _____

Timeline to complete YTG: [ ] This Year [ ] 3 Years [ ] 10 Years [ ] Lifetime

Goal # 13 – Be Aerobically Fit (Habit)

Reason for this Goal: The benefits of having a good aerobic base are enormous. Our body is completely transformed when we exercise aerobically. Our respiratory, heart, and circulatory systems receive benefits beyond anything you could imagine; and in many cases, beyond any drug or medicine.

The best book I've found on this topic is written by a doctor; it is called *Younger Next Year*, which goes into the science behind how your body is transformed. He basically says that if you exercise a minimum of 30 minutes a day for the rest of your life, you will be providing the greatest gift to yourself that you could provide, and also be able to ski and golf well into your eighties. Read this book, and you'll have all the knowledge and motivation you need to begin (or continue) your exercise regime.

Suggested Target Goal: Exercise hard for 30 minutes, 5 times a week, for one year.

Outrageous Goal: Exercise daily for the rest of your life.

My wife and I exercise 5 days/week, at 5:30am each work day, using the fitness videos available for free on YouTube, by a couple running a program called *Fitness Blender*. We love these workouts, which feature a variety of fitness routines of varying lengths, covering all aspects of fitness, including cardio fitness, using cardio exercises; high intensity interval training (HIIT), and weight lifting. It feels especially good to work up a sweat when working aerobically, knowing that your body is being put through its paces.

Your Goals:

Your Target Goal (YTG): _____

Your Outrageous Goal: _____

Timeline to complete YTG: [ ] This Year [ ] 3 Years [ ] 10 Years [ ] Lifetime

Goal # 14 – Be Strong – Lift Weights (Habit)

Reason for this Goal: Be strong by lifting weights is the best way to create a body that will perform for you throughout your life, and to help sculpt a body that you will be proud of. It's not just for bodybuilders. Lifting weights, as you get older, ensures that your bones stay strong. You send signals to your body that you are still growing, instead of the alternative of decaying. The feeling you have when your body is rebuilding itself after working out with weights is a natural high in itself. The best reasons I've come across for lifting weights, from a physiological standpoint, are explained in the book, *Younger Next Year*, by Chris Crowley. Some of the many benefits include . . .
Improves how you look and feel

- Improves whole body metabolism, aiding fat loss
- Reduces feelings of depression
- Fights osteoporosis (loss of bone mass)
- Improves your performance in sports
- Improves your overall heart health
- Improved balance and reduced risk of falling as you age
- Results in a lean and fit body, not big and bulky
- Improves your mental health

Everyone should be lifting weights. My daughter, who is currently 24 years old, lifts weights frequently, and loves it.

Suggested Target Goal: Lift weights a minimum of once a week for one year.

Outrageous Goal: Lift weights every week for the rest of your life.

You can join a gym, or just purchase a set of nested dumbbells and work out at home to a workout routine, such as by Fitness Blender.

Your Target Goal (YTG): _____

Your Outrageous Goal: _____

Timeline to complete YTG: [ ] This Year [ ] 3 Years [ ] 10 Years [ ] Lifetime

Goal # 15 – Develop a Calm Mind (Habit)

Reason for this Goal: Being able to control your mind and put it into a calm state every day is one of the best things you can do.   It is the equivalent of exercising your body, but it's for your mind.   It is especially important if you live a stressful life (Who doesn't?).

Some ideas for developing a calm mind . . .

*   Take deep, long breaths, in through the nose and out through your mouth.
*   Go for a nature walk, fade into your environment, and just listen.
*   Stop and focus on all your body senses.
*   Listen to soft instrumental music.
*   Join a Yoga class.
*   Focus on reducing your heart rate; try to get it down as low as it will go by slowing your breathing.
*   Try progressive muscle relaxation, tensing and then releasing your muscles in groups, from your head to your toes.
*   Practice mindfulness, being aware of your thoughts, without judgement.

Suggested Target Goal: Spend 10 minutes doing *nothing,* daily, for one year.

Outrageous Goal: Practice having a calm mind throughout your life.
In my twenties, I learned meditation and Tai Chi through my Karate Sensei. Daily meditation was common for me back then. In my thirties, I would go to nature—either a park, forest, or lake—and find time to reflect quietly with a calm mind. I would also sit in my car, at a park or lake at lunch time, and find this quiet time.

Your Goals:

Your Target Goal (YTG): _____

Your Outrageous Goal: _____

Timeline to complete YTG: [ ] This Year [ ] 3 Years [ ] 10 Years [ ] Lifetime

Goal # 16 – Learn How to Prepare Healthy Meals

Reason for this Goal: There are few things more satisfying than enjoying a great meal prepared at home using your own hands and your own favourite recipes. With the rise of obesity and health issues around the world, more people are resorting to eating prepared foods and fast food restaurant meals. It is becoming more important to develop the habit to prepare healthy meals at home. Eating home cooked meals with your family, around the family dinner table, is an important part of raising a successful family; and, done in a healthy manner, contributes to improving the overall health for you and your family. Some thoughts around learning how to prepare/cook healthy meals . . .

- Read books on how to cook and prepare meals.
- Take a course on how to cook and prepare meals.
- Visit a natural health store that offers lessons on food preparation and healthy eating.
- Purchase recipe books from leading chefs you admire.
- Watch TV programs on food networks.
- Make a list of your favourite foods that will form the basis of your meals.

My wife, Kathy, prepares great meals at home for our family and loves trying new recipes to keep food interesting. One of my daughters has also developed an interest in preparing healthy meals, too, as part of eating well. In reviewing this book, *100 Life Goals*, it was at the recommendation of my family that I replace one of my top 10 health and fitness goals, with this goal dedicated to learning how to cook. I instantly knew they were right.

Suggested Target Goal: Learn how to prepare 10 healthy meals for your family.

Outrageous Goal: Prepare and publish a family cookbook, with recipes of your family's top 25 favourite family meals.

Your Target Goal (YTG): _____

Your Outrageous Goal: _____

Timeline to complete YTG: [ ] This Year [ ] 3 Years [ ] 10 Years [ ] Lifetime

Goal # 17 – Learn Self-Defence

Reason for this Goal: Being able to protect yourself (self-defence) in a situation where you are being confronted or attacked could just save your life. Taking self-defence classes and/or learning a martial art to develop your self- defence skills has numerous benefits beyond protecting yourself. Being able to protect yourself is your ultimate way to preserve your health and your life. Some of the benefits derived from learning a martial art include:

* Improving your overall physical health
* Improving your confidence and projection of confidence, such that you won't be a target in the first place
* Increasing your flexibility through stretching
* Improving your reaction time
* Learning how to avoid dangerous situations in the first place

There are many self-defence programs and martial arts—which will teach you all of the skills and provide the benefits noted above—such as Karate, Taekwondo, Jujitsu, Aikido, Judo, Boxing, Kickboxing, and Mixed Martial Arts. Finding the right program comes down to finding out what martial arts studios exist within your neighbourhood or city, and choosing, based on which martial art appeals to you, with a heavy emphasis on finding the martial art that has the best teacher to teach you this important life skill.

Suggested Target Goal: Take martial arts lessons weekly for 1 year.

Outrageous Goal: Earn your black belt in a martial art, and train for life.
I joined a Karate club in my early twenties and trained 2–3x/week for 7 years, working my way through the belt system and achieving my 2nd degree Black Belt. For me, Karate became a way of life and taught me so much more than just how to defend myself. My Karate Sensei became my mentor and led me to the field of personal development, and a desire to become a better person.

Your Target Goal (YTG) :_____

Your Outrageous Goal: _____

Timeline to complete YTG: [ ] This Year [ ] 3 Years [ ] 10 Years [ ] Lifetime

Goal # 18 – Complete an Endurance or Event

Reason for this Goal: Improving your heart and aerobic health to the point that you can complete an endurance event is a great way to motivate you. An endurance race can be associated with long distance running, an ultramarathon, an adventure race, or an endurance foot race.

Choose an event or sport that already motivates you, whether it be long distance running, biking, swimming, rowing, or one of the numerous other sports, such as what you'd watch in the summer or winter Olympics. Select a distance for both target and outrageous goals that challenge you or seem outrageous or impossible. Give yourself ample time to work up to this event, such as 5 years or 1 decade, or more. We're talking about lifetime goals, remember. Some examples of endurance events you can consider include:

- A local 5Km or 10Km run
- Marathon
- Triathlon
- Tough Mudder, or one of the many other obstacle events
- Ironman (outrageous goal)

There are hundreds or thousands of events worldwide that you could get inspired to set as your goal. Spend some time researching before deciding, unless you already know precisely which event is right for you.

Another great way to *test* your physical and mental stamina is through entering into one of the numerous endurance/obstacle events, which have been created in the last few years and are taking the world by storm, many of which involve mud.

- Spartan Race
- Warrior Dash
- Mudderella
- Tough Mudder

Entering in one of these events will challenge you to get into top physical and mental condition before entering, and will provide an amazing experience with likeminded friends who you have persuaded to join you. No matter which event you choose, you will walk away a changed person, with new found confidence and courage that you can apply to your everyday life. It is a great goal to aspire to as you develop your overall health and fitness. I completed the Tough Mudder event with my sister, daughter, brother in-law, and my niece and her boyfriend. I've got to say that it was the *toughest* and *muddiest* thing I've ever done in my life, and the feeling of accomplishment afterwards was unmatched by anything I've experienced.

Suggested Target Goal: Run a 5Km local.

Outrageous Goal: Complete an Ironman competition.

I generally don't like running and have never been an endurance athlete. For me, just completing a local 5Km distance run is a big achievement. I have a friend, Dave, who has completed multiple Ironman competitions, and that is my outrageous goal.

Research the events that come to your area, and pick the one that you get most excited about. Choose to organize a group of friends, family, or work colleagues, and experience team building at its finest.

Your Goals:

Your Target Goal (YTG): _____

Your Outrageous Goal: _____

Timeline to complete YTG: [ ] This Year [ ] 3 Years [ ] 10 Years [ ] Lifetime

Goal # 19 – Play a Sport

Reason for this Goal: In terms of health and fitness, playing a sport is one of the best activities, combining physical activity by either an individual or team competing against each other, with entertainment value (competing with or against your friends). There are so many benefits derived from playing sports, and there are literally hundreds of sports to choose from, suitable for all ages. Some benefits include:

- Improved health and fitness.
- Development of social and team skills.
- Increasing the enjoyment factor of staying fit.
- Developing lifelong friendships.
- Advancing in your sport to higher competitive levels, at the regional, national, and international levels.
- Taking you to places you've never been before.
- Being beneficial to academic achievement and higher levels of confidence.

In case you're wondering what sports you could participate in, below is a partial list of different sport classifications, to get you thinking about it:

- Athletics (cross country, jumping, throwing, etc.)
- Endurance sports (running, cycling, rowing, swimming, etc.)
- Equine sports (dressage, hunter, jumper, rodeo, etc.)
- Goal sports (basketball, football, handball, etc.)
- Gymnastics (acrobatic, artistic, rhythmic, trampoline, etc.)
- Martial arts (Karate, Taekwondo, Kendo, etc.)
- Racquet sports (badminton, racquetball, squash, tennis, etc.)
- Skating sports (figure skating, roller skating, hockey, etc.)
- Strength sports (weight lifting, wrestling, rock climbing, etc.)
- Snow sports (snowboarding, skiing, etc.)
- Target sports (archery, bowling, golf, etc.)
- Wind sports (sailing, windsurfing, parachuting, etc.)

Suggested Target Goal: Play a sport.

Outrageous Goal: Play multiple sports throughout your entire life until the day you die.

In my life, the sports I've been involved with include Karate, racquetball, tennis, volleyball, and baseball; and through the involvement of my children, rhythmic gymnastics, and equestrian. Currently, I'm not involved in a competitive sport, but my children, Karah and Maddie, are (volleyball and equestrian, respectively). My plan is to take Canada's national sport of hockey and join an old timer's league, inspired by a good friend of mine, Tim, whose Dad is 80 years old and still playing hockey. If you look around carefully, there are people in their 60s, 70s, and 80s, still involved in sport. There is no reason why we can't all live an active life well beyond what most people consider to be their active ages, through their 50s. I plan to ski into my eighties and parachute on my 90th birthday. Get inspired by all the benefits sport can provide, and stay involved your entire life.

Your Goals:

Your Target Goal (YTG): _____

Your Outrageous Goal: _____

Timeline to complete YTG: [ ] This Year [ ] 3 Years [ ] 10 Year [ ] Lifetime

Goal # 20 – Develop a Long-Life Mindset

Reason for this Goal: Life is a gift. There are so many wonderful things to do, be, have, and experience in your life, and the setting of your *100 Life Goals* is just the beginning. Why not set a goal to live a long and healthy life? With the power of your mind being such a significant influencer in what you will achieve in your lifetime, the mere act of setting this goal, and believing in it, will help you live longer, so that you have as much time to experience as many things and goals as possible.

I've noticed that most people, when asked how long they plan on living, do not expect to live to an old age, nor desire to do so. They associate poor health with their later years. My perspective and challenge to you is to set an expectation that you will live not only a long life but live in such a way that your long life will be accompanied with great health until your last days.

In addition to the earlier goals that will all help your longevity, other recognized strategies to live longer include:

- Eating less (There is ample evidence to support the science behind this, related to metabolic processes.)
- Learning to breathe deeper (to increase the percentage of blood oxygen circulating through your body)
- Increasing your sleep quality (consistent, uninterrupted, full sleep cycles)
- Having a strong sense of purpose
- Being socially active
- Worrying less

Suggested Target Goal: Live healthy to age 80.

Outrageous Goal: Live healthy to age 100.

I've have had a goal since the age of 30: I firmly expect to live to the ripe old age of 100 years old. I expect to ride a bicycle on my 90th birthday. Will I achieve this goal . . . who knows? I've seen several gurus in the health field (who teach how to live a long life) die early; so there are no guarantees. If I don't make it, I'm fully accepting of that, knowing that I've fully lived and achieved so many well-planned goals, with so many good friend and family experiences. But I firmly believe I will live longer and healthier as a result of setting this goal and believing in it. I also have a long-time perspective and am more apt to take care of my health and wealth so that I'm able to enjoy my latter years actively.

One of the best books on longevity that I've come across is, *The Blue Zones: Lessons for Living Longer, From the People Who've Lived the Longest,"* written by Dan Buettner. This book studies the world's longest living people, and finds out the things in common with centenarians around the world.

At the time of writing this book, I've been reading about the potential, within the next 1 or 2 decades, for lifespans to be significantly extended due to research and advances in health care and life extensions. There are some people speculating that within our lifetime, people may live an additional 10, 20, 50, or even another 100 years! Who knows what the future holds, but it's exciting to think that if we look after our health and bodies, we may be able to live an even longer life and accomplish even more goals!

Your Goals:

Your Target Goal (YTG): _____

Your Outrageous Goal: _____

Timeline to complete YTG: [ ] This Year [ ] 3 Years [ ] 10 Years [ ] Lifetime

FAMILY AND FRIEND GOALS

Out of all the 10 Goal Areas, this is arguably one of the most important areas. We are all social beings and can only thrive and survive with close relationships with our friends and family. Our very existence depends upon on it and, as we reach our later years in life, having people who love us is all that we care about. Much of whom we become is shaped by our family beginnings and by our close social circle that we associate with. There are numerous goals that could be established in this area. I've selected goals that mainly relate to being a *good* friend or family member, something that you can't take for granted. It is important that we treat those closest to us as the most important people in our lives.

My 10 goals in this important area are:

- Choose good friends.
- Find your life partner.
- Treat your partner as a VIP.
- Go out on regular date nights.
- Learn how to be a good parent.
- Be there for your children.
- Have regular family meetings.
- Establish annual family traditions.
- Be a good friend.
- Be a good son/daughter and sibling.

Adopt, modify, or change these 10 goals to make them your own.

Goal # 21 – Choose Food Friends

Reason for this Goal: It is said that we will be as successful in life as the average of the 5 or 6 closest friends whom we associate with the most. Ensure that you develop long and lasting friendships with people of substance: people who inspire you to be your best, are good role models for you, and who always encourage you to live the life you deserve. A negative friend will impact your thoughts and your attitudes, both of which are critical. Without realizing it, spending quality time with people who don't have the characteristics of whom you'd like to be will drag you down.

You do have the power to decide who you will spend quality time with. You can't choose your family, but you can choose your friends. You can be the one that reaches out to acquaintances who inspire you and have the potential to become lifelong friends. Decide how many good friend relationships you wish to maintain in your life, and work at nurturing these relationships. Being a good friend takes effort, but it's worth it. Write out a list of all the people you consider to be your friends and acquaintances, and decide which ones you would like to have in your inner circle of closest friends. Spend the most time with these friends.

Studies prove that the success you achieve in life will be highly factored on whom you associate with. If you want to improve your chance for success and live a goal-inspired life, you need to find likeminded individuals to be part of your inner circle. List out the 5 closest people in your life, and ask yourself if you are living a life as the average of these 5 people, summed up. There is a good chance that your life will be a complete reflection of these people in terms of your overall success . . . your overall financial position, your overall health, your overall ambition, etc. If you would like to expand what you see is possible for yourself, look to replace or expand your *inner circle* with those who are the type of person you'd like to become.

A great way to stay in contact with your friends is to establish an annual getaway. I know many people who have established such a tradition with friends, which is a great way to keep in contact with friends you would otherwise grow apart from, either because of distance or busy lives.

Some ideas for friend getaways:

- A cottage weekend with just the guys or ladies
- A skiing weekend at a chalet
- A golfing tournament
- A shopping getaway
- A weekend to an entertainment city, like Las Vegas or New York
- A major concert or sporting event getaway each year
- A trip to an annual convention (comic, sporting, hunting, cottage, etc.) (There are hundreds of annual conventions to choose from.)

Suggested Goal(s):   Develop and maintain close relationships with 3-5 good friends.

Your Outrageous Goal: Spend meaningful time with your closest friends, every month, for the rest of your life.

Your Goals:

Your Target Goal (YTG): _____

Your Outrageous Goal: _____

Timeline to complete YTG: [ ] This Year [ ] 3 Years [ ] 10 Year [ ] Lifetime

Goal # 22 – Find Your Life Partner

Reason for this Goal: One of the great achievements in life is to find and commit to your ideal partner. With a loving partner, you can have and raise a family (if you choose), and live a life that you create together. Use these *100 Life Goals* as a guide for designing the life you desire. Your partner will be a constant source of love, encouragement, and companionship.

I'm no expert, but the following are some of the things many look for in finding their partner:

- Someone you're emotionally connected to
- Someone you are physically attracted to
- Someone who shares similar values in terms of
- Wanting children
- Compatible financial habits
- Someone who has good core values, like honesty and integrity
- Someone who can make you smile when you're feeling down
- Someone with whom you are comfortable communicating and sharing intimate thoughts

Some people say that opposites attract, and that may be true. The truth is that you want to have someone who has different characteristics, hobbies, and personality than yourself but with similar values. Celebrate your commonalities AND your differences.

Suggested Goal(s):   Find and marry your ideal partner.

Your Outrageous Goal: Have a happy relationship, and stay married to the same person your entire life.

I've had the great fortune of marrying my wife, Kathy, in April 1991; and we've had a great relationship for more than 25 years, raising two beautiful children, Karah and Maddie. We have many things we share in common, including our love for family, travel, old homes, being responsible with our money, playing cards, date nights, reading good books, and relaxing at our cottage or on a beach somewhere warm.

Once you find your ideal partner, work at keeping your relationship strong. Many of the habits in this coming section are written to help ensure that you maintain a healthy focus on staying happy together.

Your Goals:

Your Target Goal (YTG): _____

Your Outrageous Goal: _____

Timeline to complete YTG: [ ] This Year [ ] 3 Years [ ] 10 Years [ ] Lifetime

Goal # 23 – Treat Your Partner as a VIP (Habit)

Reason for this Goal: When you first meet your significant other, you both put your best foot forward; as you are deeply in love, you treat each other with high levels of respect, admiration, and kindness. You listen to each other attentively. You also celebrate and appreciate the differences you share (opposites attract). As you progress through your relationship or marriage, many lose focus on what brought them together in the first place. The same level of admiration and attention dwindles, and you start wanting the other person to be more like yourself. Relationships suffer. All relationships take work and effort to stay strong. Once you've made the decision that this person is your life partner (often resulting in marriage), you are making the commitment that they are the most important person in your life. They need to be treated that way, as if they are a VIP . . . Very Important Person.

Recognize the reality of what happens in many relationships, with over a third of marriages ending in divorce. Decide that you aren't going to end up in that statistic and, more importantly, decide that you will maintain an excellent relationship throughout.

Make a bold decision that your life partner will be, and will remain, your most important person throughout your life. Back it up daily with the way you interact with each other. Continue to do the things that you did when you were courting each other. Some examples on VIP treatment include:

- Establish a regular date night (see next goal).
- Listen and really talk to each other.
- Encourage your partner to pursue their own hobbies and passions
- Read books and develop your own relationship guidelines.

Suggested Goal(s): I will treat my spouse/partner as a VIP.

Your Outrageous Goal: Same as above for your entire life.

Your Target Goal (YTG): _____

Your Outrageous Goal: _____

Timeline to complete: [ ] For ever   [ ] _____

Goal # 24 – Go Out on Regular Date Nights (Habit)

Reason for this Goal: When you started dating your significant other, you likely went out on *dates*.   Once you've been together for a long time, the number of dates usually dwindles significantly, or stops.   Since your partner is to be treated as a VIP (prior goal), one of the best ways to do that is to keep the focus on dating by having a regular date night.   Keep the romance alive, and give yourselves something to look forward to each week or each month.

My wife and I have a regular date, Wednesday night, each week. We've been doing this for years now, and we both look forward to it. We either choose a restaurant or a movie, or sometimes both. It doesn't have to cost a lot of money if you are early on in your careers.   Some examples of where to go on your date include:

*   Dining at a restaurant (alternate who selects the restaurant)
*   Going to a movie (find a theatre that has a cheap movie night)
*   Attending a concert, music performance, or live show
*   Going on a hike, or strolling along the waterfront and having an ice-cream

Suggested Goal(s): Establish a date night, once a week/month.

Your Outrageous Goal: Continue date nights for the rest of your life, and spend extra time planning to make each date night extra memorable or unique.

Your Goals:

Your Target Goal (YTG): _____

Your Outrageous Goal: _____

Timeline to complete YTG: [ ] This Year [ ] 3 Years [ ] 10 Years [ ] Lifetime

Goal # 25 – Learn How to be a Good Parent (Habit)

Reason for this Goal: The most important role we have in life is that of being a parent to our children, but how much training do we actually have on this most important subject? Taking some time and setting a goal to learn how to be a good parent is vitally important, especially during the formative years of a child's life. The following are examples of areas in a child's life in which consistent parenting skills are highly desirable:

* Encouraging a child to develop social skills
* Having guidelines for watching TV and using social media
* Establishing proper eating habits/guidelines
* Knowing how to handle a child when they misbehave
* Encouraging good behaviour
* Balancing being a parent versus a friend
* Raising children who have good confidence

There are a number of ways to learn how to be a good parent:

* Read parenting books and find the author who best resonates with the parenting style you'd like to emulate.
* Take a parenting class or classes.
* Interview parents who have already raised great children and seem to have an ideal family life.
* Join a local parenting group or club.

Suggested Goal(s): Develop and agree to 7 parenting guidelines.

Your Outrageous Goal: Raise children who go on to lead amazing lives. Make a conscious decision that parenting will not be left to chance. If you've decided that you don't want your own children, learn to be great role models for the children in your life, like nieces and nephews.

Your Target Goal (YTG): _____

Your Outrageous Goal: _____

Timeline to complete YTG: [ ] Prior to 1st child being born [ ] _____

Goal # 26 – Be There For Your Children (Habit)

Reason for this Goal: If and when you decide to have children, while everyone would agree that spending quality time with your children should be at the top of your priority list, in many families, this is not the case. Too much focus on growing your career or other priorities can often have a negative impact on your ability to *be there* for your children during the important times. Ensure that you are a parent who can look back and say that you . . .

- Attended special school presentations or award ceremonies
- Met your children's teachers
- Read to your children before bed time and tucked them into bed
- Were at their extracurricular activities, games, sporting events, and performances
- Had dinner with them at least 2–3 nights throughout the week
- Actively participated in their special days, like birthdays and holidays
- Were there to listen to their challenges, and provided a comforting ear
- Celebrated their good times and bad

Your children will be so much better off for having you actively present in their life. Deciding that this is an important goal is the start. Writing it down makes this a commitment that you'll remember. Thinking about this every day will ensure that you look for the opportunities to *be there* in your children's lives, not just physically but mentally and emotionally too.

If your decision is to not have children, have this goal apply to another friend or family member.

Suggested Goal(s): Spend 1 hour a day with your children, distraction free.

Your Outrageous Goal: Be present for every special moment in your children's lives.

Your Target Goal (YTG): _____

Your Outrageous Goal: _____

Timeline to complete YTG: [ ] 1 Year [ ] Lifetime [ ] _____

Goal # 27 – Have Regular Family Meetings (Habit)

Reason for this Goal: Businesses find it important, and even essential, to have meetings to discuss important topics that are better discussed face to face. Your family life is equally and, in fact, more important than your business life, with just as many important things, and decisions to be made that impact your life. Scheduling or having regular family meetings is a great way to improve communication within your family, and a good way to plan your life and discuss these goals.

Things to discuss at family meetings include:

- Calendar of events for the coming week/month
- Family responsibilities and even distribution of chores
- Travel schedules of family members
- Children's activity schedules (games, performances, events, etc.)
- Weekend planning
- Good things that have happened
- Any needed areas of improvement (e.g., keeping the house tidy, controlling fighting amongst siblings, etc.)
- Family vacation planning
- Life goals!

Suggested Goal(s): Have regular monthly family meetings.

Your Outrageous Goal: Have regular monthly family meetings for life.

Choose which family member is best to facilitate this family meeting, and come up with a regular *agenda* of topics that are discussed each meeting, just like a business meeting. An informal and fun way to have family meetings is to schedule a weekly family dinner night, in which these topics are discussed while dining out.

Your Target Goal (YTG): _____

Your Outrageous Goal: _____

Timeline to complete YTG: [ ] This Year [ ] 3 Years [ ] 10 Years [ ] Lifetime

Goal # 28 – Establish Annual Family Traditions

Reason for this Goal: Many of life's most important things and cherished memories come from annual family traditions. While these may not seem important at the time, these traditions are what create the framework for a good family life, where children will grow up to continue these traditions and create new ones.

Examples of traditions that people cherish include:

- Cutting down a Christmas tree together
- Going to a friend's or family's cottage, the same time each year
- The hosting of a specific holiday at the same family household
- Going to a certain restaurant to celebrate someone's birthday
- Going to a local pumpkin farm every Thanksgiving
- Going to a major festival or fair each year
- Having a specific meal or restaurant outing following a specific sporting competition or event
- Singing carols together on Christmas Eve

It's during these annual traditions that you spend important time together with parents, siblings, extended family members, and friends. Ensure that you make the time and recognize the importance of nurturing these relationships.

Suggested Goal(s): Establish your own annual family traditions.

Your Outrageous Goal: Continue your family traditions for life.

If you don't currently have any (or many) family traditions, consciously think about what you'd like to start . . . and repeat each year!

Your Target Goal (YTG): _____

Your Outrageous Goal: _____

Timeline to complete YTG: [ ] This Year [ ] 3 Years [ ] 10 Years [ ] Lifetime

Goal # 29 – Be a Good Friend

Reason for this Goal: Good relationships with just a few close friends is really important. It's easy to have many acquaintances whom we call friends, but it takes more to be a good or best friend. A good friend will be there through the good times and the bad, throughout your entire life, to grow old with. A good friend is someone who . . .

* Likes you because of you, and not because of your *status* in life
* You can talk to about anything
* Is honest and will tell you what they really think when you're about to make a key life decision
* Doesn't need to schedule a time to see you; they'll just swing by
* Is part of your important events in life
* Is dependable and keeps his or her word
* Is loyal and keeps your confidence, standing by your side through thick and thin
* You like to be around, and they will try to cheer you up if needed
* You have "life is good" moments with regularly
* Is forgiving and doesn't hold grudges
* You are comfortable being around, regardless of what is going on

If you don't currently have friends whom you would call good friends, as characterized above, decide that you will seek them out. Remember the importance of having friends that are good people (reference Goal 21). Also remember that it takes work and effort to be a good friend, but it is vitally important.

Man has evolved through the centuries in tribes as social beings, so why is it that so many of us have limited meaningful social connections, and face loneliness. In the book, *Blue Zones,* about the longest living centenarians on this planet, one of the common factors is that people with good social connections are the happiest and live the longest.

As we move on in life, it is so easy to lose contact with friends and acquaintances of all kinds, especially friends from our different schools that we have attended: public school, high school, college, or university.

It takes effort to stay in contact. Be the person that reaches out. Don't worry if the other person doesn't reciprocate; that doesn't mean they don't want to stay in contact.

Kathy and I are very fortunate to have had an amazing best friend relationship with the couple that introduced the two of us back in the late 1980s. Gary and Sue have been part of our life in so many ways:

- Best Man and Maid of Honor at our wedding in 1991
- Purchased a park model trailer together at a recreational resort in 2004
- Annual getaways to Niagara Falls or Niagara On the Lake
- Cottage getaways
- I was Master of Ceremonies at their 25th wedding anniversary celebration
- Multiple trips to Maui together

We also have great relationships with two other couples, with whom we travel together and enjoy each other's company immensely, both of whom we've taken cruises with.

Suggested Goal(s):   Maintain at least 2 good friend relationships.

Your Outrageous Goal: Maintain 10 good friend relationships.

Your Goals:

Your Target Goal (YTG): _____

Your Outrageous Goal: _____

Timeline to complete YTG: [ ] This Year [ ] 3 Years [ ] 10 Years [ ] Lifetime

Goal # 30 – Be a Good Son, Daughter, Sibling

Reason for this Goal: Our parents are responsible for bringing us into this world and for dedicating much of their life to raising us. It is important that we recognize the importance of our parents throughout our lives, and be there for them, not just while growing up but as they age. The same goes for our siblings (brothers and sisters) as we grow up together.

Some ideas for being a good son, daughter, or sibling:

* Listen to and respect your parents.
* Help them with chores around the house.
* Enjoy family meals together.
* Honor family traditions.
* Spend time with them for no reason.
* Learn their history and story of their lives, for future generations.
* Recognize them on all birthdays, holidays, and special occasions.
* Travel together and enjoy their company.
* Involve them in your children's lives.
* Support them in their senior years with health and financial needs.

Some people develop grievances with their parents and/or siblings, which develop into not seeing them. Work hard to remove any challenges that exist with your parents and siblings so that you can continue to support each other throughout your adult lives. You only have one family, and it is important for you to recognize and care for them. At the end of their, and your, life, it is these relationships that are among the most important, and could be the only things that matter.

Suggested Goal(s): Have a great relationship with your parents and siblings.

Your Outrageous Goal: Be there for your parents and siblings your entire life.

Your Target Goal (YTG): _____

Your Outrageous Goal: _____

Timeline to complete YTG: [ ] This Year [ ] 3 Years [ ] 10 Years [ ] Lifetime

HOBBIES AND PASSONS

This Goal area is one of the most important areas in terms of living a life that is uniquely you. There are literally hundreds (or even thousands) of hobbies, passions, and loves that you can get involved with. As parents, our goal is to expose our children to as many of these as possible, in the hope that they will find something that they become passionate above. As adults, we become so engaged with our other responsibilities (family, career, etc.) that we sometimes stop doing the things that we were once so passionate about. In retirement, we all of a sudden have enough time to immerse ourselves in past and new hobbies, taking them to a new level.

To live a life that is meaningful and exciting, you need to either discover or rediscover things that you can devote meaningful time to. The following list is just the tip of the iceberg in terms of things that can become your hobbies, passions, and loves:

- Animals: equestrian, pets, animal care
- Automotive: cars, motorcycles
- Church: religion, spirituality, volunteering
- Creative: painting, crafts, sewing, photography
- Home: renovations, restorations, interior decorating
- Indoors: reading, TV, movies, games, computers
- Music: playing, entertaining, live music, concerts
- Outdoors: fishing, gardening, hunting, camping, boating
- Sports: golfing, swimming, skiing, tennis
- Social Activities: bowling, billiards, curling, dancing

Try writing out a list of everything that you have done in your life or aspire to do in your life, which you believe you have a passion for. If you want to dive further into this, the best way is to follow Raymond Aaron's annual *Love Letters* approach, as described in his book, *Double Your Income Doing What You Love,* where he teaches an approach, and provides a detailed template to do this.

These next pages are designed so that you can completely develop goals around the things that make you . . . you!   When you've completed these 10 goals, expand the number to 100, and keep going.

As an example, the following is a sample of the hobbies and passions I have at this stage of my life, outside of the balanced goals written about in this book . . .

Hobby, Passion, or Love

* Going to concerts/listening to music
* Coastal drives
* Playing guitar
* Traveling
* Exploring quaint towns and villages
* Historic buildings and architecture
* Weekend getaways
* Hiking
* Cottage life
* Dancing
* Playing the drums
* Skiing
* Bicycling
* Karate/martial arts
* Attending success conferences
* Real Estate
* Exploring waterfronts with piers
* Dining in great restaurants
* Watching music talent competitions

Start by making your own list of all those things that you love. Don't filter anything out; just write what comes to mind. You don't have to follow through with writing goals for everything you've written down. Just create a master list to start with.

List Your Hobbies or Passions Here

-
-
-
-
-
-
-
-
-
-
-
-
-
-
-
-
-
-
-
-
-
-
-
-
-
-
-
-
-
-
-
-
-
-
-

Goals # 31 – 40

Enter your Hobbies and Passion goals here (sample goals).

#	Target Goal	Outrageous Goal	Timeline*
31	Do an annual nature hike with my family.	Hike all the local trails within a 100Km radius	10 years
32	Take an annual ski vacation	Keep skiing well in to my eighties	Start next year
33	Take dance lessons with my spouse	Enter a dance competition	3 years
34	Take photography lessons	Have my photographs published	3 years
35	Learn a musical instrument, or to sing	Play live in a band at a public paid performance	5 years
36	Buy a boat	Spend an entire summer on my boat	10 years
37	Ride a bicycle more than 100Km in a single day	Ride my bicycle around Lake Ontario	10 years
38	Raise $10,000 for charity	Raise $1M for charity	20 years
39	Learn to golf	Learn to golf well with no handicap	5 years
40	Learn another language	Learn 2 or more additional languages	10 years

Enter your Hobbies and Passions here.

#	Target Goal	Outrageous Goal	Timeline*
31			
32			
33			
34			
35			
36			
37			
38			
39			
40			

*Timeline for achieving target goal.

FINANCIAL GOALS

Understanding how money works and how to develop your financial worth is essential to living your life of WOW. While money is not everything, and being obsessed about money is bad, most people agree that having enough financial wealth to live a comfortable lifestyle is important. And depending upon the type of goals you set for yourself, considerable financial net worth may be required. The purpose of this chapter is to help you understand the need to learn about money, and to track it, and do things to increase your income and the growth of your asset base, so that you do have the financial resources to live the life you dream of. My following 10 goals are designed to do just that.

- Learn personal finance 101
- Learn a financial tool to manage your money
- Develop a budget and track your cash flow
- Develop a good credit rating
- Track and develop your net worth
- Invest 10% of your income
- Find a good financial adviser / mentor
- Own investment real estate
- Increase your income
- Plan your retirement

It is important that you learn as much as you can about personal finance, and develop, early on, good financial habits that will last throughout your life time. Examples of good financial habits include avoiding consumer debt and buying things that you can't afford to buy with cash in the bank. If you use credit cards, pay off the full balance each month.

- Don't try to *keep up with the Joneses.* They are likely deep in debt.
- Live more frugally in the first part of your life when you are setting up your asset base for long-term growth (see Goals # 42 and 47).
- In a 2-person household, live on one income and save or invest the other.
- Use *good debt* to buy assets that appreciate (i.e. real estate, stocks).
- Read the book, *The Millionaire Next Door*, for the results of a comprehensive study on who really has wealth (It's not who you think.).

Goal # 41 – Learn Personal Finance 101

Reason for this Goal: Once you graduate from school and start living on your own, your ability to understand and manage your money will have a massive impact on the rest of your life. If you're like most people, you've had very little formal education on how money works and how to manage it. Either you learn to manage your money, or money will manage you.

Whether you're still in your teenage years or you're in your middle years, it's not too late to understand money, but the earlier you learn is definitely better. Make it an important goal to learn about money and how to earn and grow it. Some of the things you will want to learn about include:

- Different types of income
- The magic of compound interest
- Your credit rating and why it's important
- The difference between good debt and bad debt
- Mortgages and what you need to know about them
- Credit cards and how to use them properly
- Taxes and some common tax strategies
- The best way to grow (invest) your money
- Why you must spend less than you earn, and avoid excess materialism
- The tools to help you track your money

This goal is not to be taken lightly. The sooner you learn about these principles, the better. It could mean the difference between you retiring broke or as a millionaire. There are hundreds, and possibly thousands, of books, teachers, and websites devoted to this. The truth is that most people do not have strong financial literacy. Don't let that be you.

Suggested Goal(s): Read a book that covers these financial topics.

Your Outrageous Goal: Teach your family and friends about personal finance.

Your Target Goal (YTG): _____

Your Outrageous Goal: _____

Timeline to complete YTG: [ ] This Year [ ] 3 Years [ ] 10 Years

Goal # 42 – Learn a Financial Management Tool

Reason for this Goal: I consider Microsoft Excel to be one of the best financial tools ever invented. Excel, in its simplest form, is a tool for entering numbers and creating formulas to add, subtract, divide, and multiply rows and columns of numbers. In its advanced form, Excel allows you to do detailed financial analysis and projections. Learning how to use Excel, or one of the other excellent tools available, is important if you are going to truly understand how money comes in and out of your life. Learning and using a financial tool will support you in your efforts to . . .

- Develop a budget to track your cash flow (your income and expenses)
- Track your assets (things you own)
- Track your liabilities (money you owe for the things you own)
- Know your net worth (your assets minus your liabilities)
- Do financial projections for the future (*what-if* scenarios)
- Analyze the difference in financial outcomes of different investment returns, including real estate
- And so much more

Most major banks, and many independent companies, offer financial tools that link to your accounts to help you manage and track your money. One of the better non-banking tools, as recommended by a financial site I frequent (www.financialsamurai.com), is by Personal Capital.

Suggested Goal(s): Learn Excel and set up your own financial tools.

Your Outrageous Goal: Develop customized financial tools of your own.
The thing I like about Excel is that it has stood the test of time, and any spreadsheets you develop now will likely be just as relevant 20 years from now.

Your Target Goal (YTG): _____

Your Outrageous Goal: _____

Timeline to complete YTG: [ ] This Year [ ] 3 Years [ ] 10 Years [ ] Lifetime

Goal # 43 – Develop a Budget and Track Your Cash Flow (Habit)

Reason for this Goal: Understanding how to budget your money so that you spend within your means is a foundational principle of money management. The tracking of your expenses (what you spend your money on) against your income (what you earn in your job or business) is important to ensuring you stay within your budget. It is easy to start spending more money than you make, and that will lead to debt problems. By inputting these financial numbers into an Excel spreadsheet, or one of the other on-line tools that are available from your bank or as a downloadable app, you will gain confidence in your spending and will have controls in place to spend within your budget.

Set up your budget and cash flow projections to track the following:

- INCOME – the pay from your employer, and income from other sources, such as a rental property, etc.
- EXPENSES – house, taxes, children, clothing, education, food, dining out, gifts, automotive, gym membership, charity, health, insurance, vacations, etc.

Your budget = your plan on what you will spend your money on.

Your cash flow = income less your expenses.

You can track your budget and cash flow on a weekly, monthly or annual basis.

Suggested Goal(s):   Develop a system for tracking your cash flow.

Your Outrageous Goal: Maintain your cash flow tracking system for life.

Your Target Goal (YTG): _____

Your Outrageous Goal: _____

Timeline to complete YTG: [ ] This Year [ ] 3 Years [ ] 10 Years [ ] Lifetime

Goal # 44 – Develop a Good Credit Rating

Reason for this Goal: Establishment of a good credit rating is important to be able to borrow money from the bank. One of the most important reasons to establish a good credit rating is to be able to finance the purchase of your first house or to start your own business.

Your credit report is a record of how you manage your credit obligations. This data is analyzed and used to calculate your credit score.

Your credit score is a number that lenders use to help them decide whether or not to extend you credit. It represents their risk assessment related to whether or not they can expect you to repay their money borrowed, according to the agreement you sign with them.

There are many places you can go to learn about credit scores, and there are courses taught by experienced professionals on how to systematically improve your credit scores. Demonstrating a solid history of paying down your credit obligations on time, such as a credit card, is part of establishing your good credit rating.

Being able to borrow money to earn money, whether through passive investments (stocks, mutual funds, etc.) or active investments (real estate, business) is important to your financial success.

Suggested Goal(s): Develop a credit score of __ or above.

Your Outrageous Goal: Maintain an A+ credit score throughout your working life.

Your Target Goal (YTG): _____

Your Outrageous Goal: _____

Timeline to complete YTG: [ ] This Year [ ] 3 Years [ ] 10 Years [ ] Lifetime

Goal # 45 – Track and Develop Your Net Worth (Habit)

Reason for this Goal: The tracking of your net worth—your assets (what you own) versus your liabilities (what you owe)—is important to growing your money. Over time, you can see the benefits of how owning productive assets, like real estate and stocks, will grow and increase your net worth. Your net worth is a good measure of how wealthy you are, and is easy to track. The tracking of your net worth will inspire you to make smart money and investment decisions that will improve your net worth throughout your life. Having a good net worth gives you the peace of mind and freedom to achieve your 100 life goals, knowing that you have the financial assets behind you to achieve your travel and lifestyle goals. By inputting these financial numbers (assets and liabilities) into an Excel spreadsheet, or one of the other on-line tools that are available from your bank or as a downloadable app, you will gain confidence in your future.

Track your net worth by setting up the following types of categories:

- ASSETS: Real Estate, Investments, Vehicles, Cash (in bank accounts), etc.
- LIABILITIES: Mortgages, Lines of Credit, Car Loans, Credit Cards, etc.

Your Net Worth = Assets minus your Liabilities. You only need to track your net worth on an annual basis once you've set up your tracking system.

One of my original 100 goals, at the age of 30, was to achieve a net worth of two million dollars—a number I determined would be sufficient to retire. Within 15 years of owning investment real estate, my wife and I developed our first one million dollars in net worth, excluding our principle residence. This massive increase in net worth, from the time I wrote out the goal, has been a significant contributor in our ability to accomplish so many of these 100 goals. Through following the principles outlined in this Financial Goals section—specifically the next 2 goals of owning investment real estate and investing 10% of our income—we have exceeded this goal and have been fortunate to have our net worth grow at a rate averaging 20% per annum, for more than 20 years.

The very act of tracking your net worth will inspire you to make good financial decisions that will allow it to grow.

Suggested Goal(s):   Develop a system for tracking your net worth.

Your Outrageous Goal: Develop a net worth of more than $X million.

Your Goals:

Your Target Goal (YTG): _____

Your Outrageous Goal: _____

Timeline to complete YTG: [ ] This Year [ ] 3 Years [ ] 10 Years [ ] Lifetime

"If you were to show me your current financial plan, would I get so excited by it that I would go across the country and lecture on it? If the answer is no, then here's my question: 'Why not?' Why wouldn't you have a superior financial plan that is taking you to the places you want to go?" – Jim Rohn

Goal # 46 – Invest 10% of Your Income - Pay Yourself First (Habit)

Reason for this Goal: The single best financial habit you could develop is to *pay yourself* first. Take 10% of each pay cheque and invest it into appreciating assets. Just like you would pay all your expenses (car, insurance, utilities, mortgage, etc.), consider the "Pay Yourself 10%" as a mandatory expense that you pay. You will be happy you start this key financial habit, as this single habit will (should) allow you to become a millionaire before the time you retire.

Besides real estate, there are other important appreciating asset classes to invest in to develop your net worth. In general, you want to buy things that go up in value (appreciate) versus things that go down in value (depreciate).

Appreciating Assets: stocks, bonds, real estate, GICs, mutual funds, index funds, silver, gold, diamonds, art, etc.

Depreciating Assets: cars, trailers, clothes, boats, ATVs, furniture, etc.

To really understand this concept of paying yourself first, read *The Wealthy Barber*, by David Chilton. This is a legendary book and a *must-read* book for all those new to investing. To understand how to invest in the stock market, read about the investing strategies of the # 1 investor of all time: billionaire, Mr. Warren Buffet. With the application of this goal, and the benefits of learning about compound interest (discussed in Goal # 41), you benefit the most by starting to invest in appreciating assets as soon as you start earning income, to have the maximum benefit of time for the compounding to work for you.

Suggested Goal(s): Put 10% of each pay into an appreciating asset account.

Your Outrageous Goal: Own > $3M in appreciating assets by retirement.

Your Target Goal (YTG): _____

Your Outrageous Goal: _____

Timeline to complete YTG: [ ] This Year [ ] 3 Years [ ] 10 Years [ ] Lifetime

Goal # 47 – Find Your Financial Mentor/Adviser

Reason for this Goal: A good financial mentor, adviser, or planner will be able to help you achieve your financial goals and ensure you remain focused to achieve your investment goals. You can also find a local investment club, or group, that specializes in buying investment real estate or investing in other asset classes, in your local area. While you can just go it alone, working with people and learning from their mistakes can save you a lot of time and costly errors. Types of financial advisors and investment clubs available are . . .

- Financial adviser (commission based)
- Financial planner (fee based)
- On-line financial services company
- An experienced, wealthy friend or mentor to guide you
- Stock, mutual fund, or bond investment club
- Private investment club

The people you associate with, who help you, will to a large degree impact your financial health. Taking the time to find the right financial mentor, advisor, investment club, or on-line financial services company is a great way to be mentored by success-minded people, and will give you the confidence to act. Good planners and investment groups will have regular meetings, training classes, monthly newsletters, and member websites for you to learn from. Make sure you consider the fees and management expense ratios associated with your financial advice, as the impacts to your financial results can be enormous.

Suggested Goal(s): Find your financial mentor or adviser, meet with them regularly, and start investing.

Your Outrageous Goal: Become a contributing member of an investment club that helps others.

Your Target Goal (YTG): _____

Your Outrageous Goal: _____

Timeline to complete YTG: [ ] This Year [ ] 3 Years [ ] 10 Years [ ] Lifetime

Goal # 48 – Own Investment Real Estate

Reason for this Goal: Of all the investment classes, real estate is the foundation of a high percentage of high net worth individuals. Because there is only a limited supply of land, and the population of the world continues to increase at record pace, real estate will continue to increase in price when viewed as a long-term investment. There are several distinct and unique advantages to owning real estate: Real estate is something the average person can understand.
You can invest in real estate while holding a full-time career, and treat it as your *side hustle*/hobby.

You can rent your real estate and have tenants pay off your debt.

Over time, you can improve your positive cash flow as rents increase at the going market rate, while your mortgage payment remains more constant (based on your mortgage term and prevailing interest rates).

By buying property in *up and coming* neighbourhoods, you can multiply your equity and cash flow gains as the desirability of living in your neighbourhood increases. You gain the benefits of controlling a very large asset, and the gains associated with it, with only a small down payment (typically 5 to 20%), such that you maximize your return on investment.

You can increase the value of your real estate through your own physical efforts of learning to do home renovations yourself instead of paying someone.

Some people strive to become millionaires to support their retirement goals. Investing in real estate for the long term is a proven way to become a millionaire, as long as you invest for the long term.

As a simple example, let's say you purchase a home or condo for $300,000, which produces a break-even cash flow.   After having your tenants pay off your mortgage over the 25 years, you will own the house outright; but after 25 years, the house is likely to be worth at least double what you paid for it.   At 5% appreciation per year (quite possible in some locations/markets), your $300,000 house will be worth more than $1,000,000.   If homes don't appreciate 5% per annum in your area, that's okay too. You will still have a substantial paid off asset when you are ready for retirement.

"Real estate cannot be lost or stolen, nor can it be carried away. Purchased with common sense, paid for in full, and managed with reasonable care, it is about the safest investment in the world." – Franklin D. Roosevelt

Owning physical real estate isn't for everyone. You need to have a certain temperament to deal with tenants and maintenance issues, or trust others to look after this for you. If you can, the payback can be tremendous! For those that can never see themselves as landlords, there are other ways to invest in real estate and still benefit, such as through lending as a silent partner in a joint venture agreement, or investing in a real estate investment trust (REIT). REITs were established for small investors not interested in the responsibilities of property maintenance or managing tenants directly, to be able to invest in real estate without the large capital required to purchase real estate directly, yet be a part owner in the underlying real estate.

I have written a book, entitled, *Buy Your Neighbours House . . . a strategy to developing wealth on your own street,* based on our success in owning our Gables on The Park properties—4 heritage homes in Canada's # 1 mid-sized city. If you are interested in more information, this book explains that there are several distinct and important advantages of owning property in close proximity to your personal residence, and how to know if it makes sense for you.

Suggested Goal(s): Buy a rental property.

Your Outrageous Goal: Own multiple investment properties.

Your Goals:

Your Target Goal (YTG): _____

Your Outrageous Goal: _____

Timeline to complete YTG: [ ] This Year [ ] 3 Years [ ] 10 Years [ ] Lifetime

Goal # 49 – Increase Your Income (Habit)

Reason for this Goal: Depending upon the goals that you are establishing for yourself, specifically in the areas of lifestyle and travel goals, it is likely that you will need to find ways to increase your income beyond your current levels. In addition to the goals within this Financial Goals category, the following are ideas on how you can increase your income:

*   Get into a good profession or career with potential to develop great income.
*   Establish a side business as a secondary income source, possibly focused on one of your life passions.
*   Start and develop your own successful business (i.e. the kinds of businesses you see pitched on television, on *Dragons Den* or *Shark Tank*).
*   Be an excellent employee (See goal # 55).
*   Develop an on-line internet marketing business.
*   Join a network marketing business.
*   Become an authority in your business area by writing a book.
*   Drive for Uber or Lyft.
*   Rent out a room in your house, on Air BNB.
*   Sell stuff on Kijiji, Craigslist, or Amazon.
*   Tutor people, in your area of passion or expertise.
*   Spend less and save more.

Early in my life, I played music in bands, which in addition to being one of my life passions, provided me with additional income. An extra $100 from a gig I played was a big deal when I was just starting out. I performed in several bands— Cartune, Dorian Wild, and Groove Doctors— performing in bars and clubs around the Greater Toronto Area as a bass player, from the 1970s to the 1990s.

I went to DeVry Institute of Technology, and I obtained my diploma as an Electronics Technologist, leading to a successful career as a proposal manager, working for one of our country's top employers in the aerospace industry. As an employee, I purchased 4 investment properties and 1 vacation property, over a period of 20 years, as a *hobby* in my spare time. This turned out to be the main key to our financial success and ability to finance our lifestyle. The excellent equity build-up and cash flow produced through buying investment real estate was enhanced by purchasing property in Ontario, one of the best growth areas in

Canada throughout the 1990s and 2000s. I encourage you to look at your own life and circumstances, and start developing a plan on how you will increase your income. Each month, do something significant that will increase your income and your net worth.

I was involved in a network marketing business for several years (Amway/ Quixtar) during my thirties. This taught me a lot about people skills and leadership, which led me to achieve significant income growth through my employer by being an excellent employee and leader (see Goals # 55 & 56).

Suggested Goal(s): Increase my income by 15-20% within 3 years.

Your Outrageous Goal: Continue to increase my income by 10% per year, for life.

Your Goals:

Your Target Goal (YTG): _____

Your Outrageous Goal: _____

Timeline to complete YTG: [ ] This Year [ ] 3 Years [ ] 10 Years [ ] Lifetime

Goal # 50 – Plan Your Retirement

Reason for this Goal: As we get older, many of us dream of one day retiring from our work and our daily grind of working 8, 9, or 10-hour days or more. Some of us just want the financial freedom to be able to live our last two or three decades on our own terms, getting up when we want and doing the things that we love to do, without worrying about having the money to do so. To be able to live past the traditional retirement age of 65, and have enough money to live well into our eighties, nineties, or beyond, will require a significant investment portfolio, depending upon the retirement lifestyle you aspire to.

One of my life goals is to live for today while planning for the future. We shouldn't think only about how life will be good some day when we retire, because you'll miss out on the real purpose of life, which is to live a life in the moment and a life of purpose. It's likely that the whole concept of retirement is not well understood. Mandatory retirement, at age 65, was introduced in Germany in the late 1800s, when people only lived to 67 years or so, to allow the younger workforce employment opportunities. More than a century later, our lifespans have increased substantially, and retirement has evolved and romanticised into living the life of leisure. Our aim is to have passions in our life, and if you really love working, you should continue to work for as long as you want.

Regardless of your view on retirement, you should plan for some day having enough money so you can live out the last 2 or 3 decades of your life such that money is not an issue for you. Using Excel or other tools, it's relatively easy to track your financial objectives using a comprehensive financial retirement plan/tracking sheet.

Suggested Goal(s):   Develop a plan for your retirement.

Your Outrageous Goal: Update your retirement plan, annually, for life.

Your Target Goal (YTG): _____

Your Outrageous Goal: _____

Timeline to complete YTG: [ ] This Year [ ] 3 Years [ ] 10 Years [ ] Lifetime

CAREER GOALS

A career is an occupation or profession, which we follow as our *life's work*, from which we generate income to be able to live. We can have many careers throughout the course of our life. For some, choosing a career is easy and natural. For others, it is difficult. As we graduate from high school, we are expected to choose our education path, which will formulate our career path. Having completed our further education (college, university, etc.), we either end up in the career we've been educated on, or we find out we can't find employment, and we move on to something else. We sometimes end up in careers that we thought we would love but then find out we don't. I believe that selecting your career is one of the most difficult decisions we all must make. And once we are in our chosen career, changing careers is one of the most difficult decisions we will ever make. My next 10 goals are designed to help you select your career, develop your career, and excel in your career.

- Do a career assessment
- Get an education
- Find or develop your passion
- Join a professional organization
- Be a good employee
- Be a good leader
- Be an expert in something
- Become an authority
- Be your own boss
- Create multiple income sources

Adopt, modify, or change these 10 goals to make them your own.

Goal # 51 – Do a Career Assessment

Reason for this Goal: In looking at our career aspirations, it's important to understand who you are as a person and what your natural strengths and weaknesses are. While everyone has the potential to grow into the person they need to become to achieve their goals, we all have different starting points, and we need to recognize where that is before we start planning our career. Questions that we need to ask (and answer) are:

- Do I know what my passions are?
- Am I an introvert or an extrovert?
- Do I like having a high level of interaction with people, or working by myself?
- Do I have good communication skills?
- Could I manage or lead other people?

There are many assessment tools that are available, which ask hundreds more questions and are designed to hone in on the type of career that is right for you.

- Myers-Briggs – Finds your distinctive personality traits among 16 types
- MyPlan.com – Identifies what's really important to you in your career
- Holland Code – Examines 6 occupational themes: Realistic, Investigative, Artistic, Social, Enterprising, and Conventional
- And more . . . find one you connect with.

Suggested Goal(s): Do a thorough self-assessment(s).

Your Outrageous Goal: Update your self-assessment every decade.

Your Goals:

Your Target Goal (YTG): _____

Your Outrageous Goal: _____

Timeline to complete YTG: [ ] This Year [ ] 3 Years [ ] 10 Years [ ] Lifetime

Goal # 52 – Get an Education

Reason for this Goal: A good education will give you the foundation for establishing your career. Unless you are an entrepreneur who will succeed regardless of education, you'll need an education—if for nothing else, as an insurance policy to ensure you get that first good job, or as a lead-up to starting your own business. Many employers won't consider you without the requisite education. They assume that a person with education:

*   Has the discipline to complete a rigorous program of study
*   Has the intelligence for the position being hired
*   Is committed to the field in which they were educated

For the majority of people, a good education is your *safety net* for ensuring you can make a living. If you want to exceed beyond making a living, it is your *self-education* that will make you a fortune. See Personal Development goals, 1–10. Based on your self-assessment and passion(s), choose from the following types of education possible for you:

*   Community college
*   University, undergraduate program
*   University, graduate program
*   Vocational school
*   Alternative education programs

If you're fortunate to know someone very successful, who is willing to mentor you directly and start you down what you think could be a great career path, then bypass the formal education; and only return to the formal education if it doesn't work out. Seek advice before going down this path, however.

Suggested Goal(s):   Get a good education.

Your Outrageous Goal: Achieve the highest level of education in your field.

Your Target Goal (YTG): _____

Your Outrageous Goal: _____

Timeline to complete YTG: [ ] This Year [ ] 3 Years [ ] 10 Years [ ] Lifetime

Goal # 53 – Find or Develop Your Passion

Reason for this Goal: To find and/or develop a life passion is to truly live your life. Some people never develop their passion. Others are living passionately. You can see it on their face, in the way they talk, walk, and smile. To find or develop passion means that . . .

- You'll never work another day in your life (because it won't seem like work).
- You will be living your life of purpose.
- You will rise to the top of your profession, naturally.
- You'll have less stress and are likely to live longer.
- You'll keep working for as long as you are able, and you'll enjoy it.

There is considerable discussion (and debate) about these 2 questions:

- Do successful people develop their personal passion into a career? This is the cornerstone of hundreds of books on success.
- Does passion and success evolve while working and developing your career to a point where you are passionate about your work? A great book, which discusses this thoroughly, is called, *Be So Good They Can't Ignore You,* by Cal Newport.

In either case, it is your mission to discover or develop your passion. If you can incorporate or develop passion into your career, then going to work each day is a privilege and something to look forward to. Countless people are in jobs and careers that they are not passionate about. Don't let that be you. Many people can develop passionate careers around a wide variety of careers, by putting in the time and effort to becoming experts in their field, which ultimately leads to passion and success.

But if you are in a career that is only just paying the bills, and you cannot feel passionate about it, pursue your passion in your non-work time. There is a chance that your personal passion could come out of your responses to the section, Goals # 31 to 40, earlier in this book.

Things to think about in determining your passion(s):

- What things do you love doing that you would do for free?
- What inspires you deeply?
- What makes your heart sing?
- What things come naturally and effortlessly?
- What do you look forward to the most?

Suggested Goal(s):   Become so good at your job that passion naturally follows.

Your Outrageous Goal: Live passionately in all that you do, including your hobbies and your career.

This is a goal that I've struggled with through much of my life; I've been influenced by so many books that have said you need to take your passion and develop a career around it. This is not easy, as most passions start off as hobbies (in my case, music and Karate) and not necessarily something you're good enough at to develop a serious career around.   After reading the book referenced above, I read an article published by Mark Cuban (billionaire featured on *Shark Tank*), and he stated, "One of the great lies of life is *follow your passions*."   His argument is that most people we deem successful did not initially follow their passion; they developed it from putting in so much time and effort that they became recognized as experts and authorities in their field. As an example, he says, if your passion is baseball, and you turn this into a career, unless you possess the natural strengths of a pro-ball player (i.e. in the case of a pitcher, being able to throw a ball at 90 MPH), you are prone to failure.

Your Goals:

Your Target Goal (YTG): _____

Your Outrageous Goal: _____

Timeline to complete YTG: [ ] This Year [ ] 3 Years [ ] 10 Years [ ] Lifetime

Goal # 54 – Join a Professional Association

Reason for this Goal: A professional association is an organization seeking to further the interests of the individuals employed in a certain field. Some of the benefits of joining and belonging to such an organization:

- Associations transform an occupation into a profession, and can establish you as an expert in your field.
- Some associations will certify you, to indicate you possess qualifications in the subject area.
- They offer opportunities for continued learning, and updating of skills.
- The organization helps self-guard public interest.
- Membership indicates to your employer, and to the people you work for or with, that you are serious about your chosen field and maintain the high standards of your profession.

Some of the hundreds of professional associations include:

- American Society of Civil Engineers (ASCE)
- Certified Management Accountant (CMA)
- Institute of Electrical and Electronics Engineers (IEEE)
- Association of Proposal Management Professionals (APMP)
- International Association of Administrative Professionals (IAAP)
- International Federation of Robotics (IFR)

Suggested Goal(s): Join a professional organization.

Your Outrageous Goal: Start your own local chapter.

Some organizations are looking to expand and develop local chapters, for which you can volunteer to lead or participate in. This will further enhance the recognition you have within your field.

Your Target Goal (YTG): _____

Your Outrageous Goal: _____

Timeline to complete YTG: [ ] This Year [ ] 3 Years [ ] 10 Years [ ] Lifetime

Goal # 55 – Be a Good Employee (Habit)

Reason for this Goal: Most of us aspire to have a successful career. While working for a company as an employee, there are things you can do to become more promotable within your company. An excellent employee is what all employers seek, and you will be rewarded for it. To be a good employee:

*   Be the one your boss depends on to get something done
*   Develop a sense of urgency for the things that your boss asks
*   Become the *go-to* person for others
*   Take advantage of opportunities to expand your knowledge
*   Become focused on continuous improvement
*   Be the person that does more than you're paid to do (within reason)
*   Look for ways to generate more income or cut costs
*   Lead without title (be a leader regardless of your position)
*   Improve your communication skills (verbal, written, speaking, etc.)

A good company and a good boss will reward you for exhibiting the above characteristics. If not, it may be time to move on. The number one reason people leave their positions at a company are because they don't feel respected or appreciated by their boss.

The best investment you can make in yourself is through becoming a better person. Self-help learning (reading, attending workshops, etc.) will help you in all areas of your life, and you should see a direct correlation to your income.

Suggested Goal(s):   Be the best employee in your department.

Your Outrageous Goal: Be promoted to a senior position within your company.

Your Target Goal (YTG): _____

Your Outrageous Goal: _____

Timeline to complete YTG: [ ] This Year [ ] 3 Years [ ] 10 Years [ ] Lifetime

Goal # 56 – Be a Good Leader (Habit)

Reason for this Goal: A good leader is sought after in all businesses and organizations, whether you are running your own business or are an employee in someone else's business. Even an employee in a junior position can exhibit leadership, and there is room within any organization for leaders to excel. Not only are leaders respected and admired, leaders have the strongest careers and more personal satisfaction in their work life.

A good piece of advice I learned is to consider yourself as the president of your own business, even while working for a company or a boss. Here are some examples of how you can exhibit leadership within your career:

- Speak up in meetings or to your boss about things that matter.
- Make suggestions on how to improve the business. Offer to help.
- Advocate for spending wisely.
- Develop your communication skills (writing, speaking, etc.). See Goal 8.
- Don't accept status quo; embrace change.
- Encourage and support goal setting within your organization.
- Don't speak badly about any individual. Be constructive.
- Treat others the way you'd like to be treated.
- Engage in crucial conversations, especially if you manage others.
- Be optimistic about the way things will be.

Suggested Goal(s): Be a good leader.

Your Outrageous Goal: Have others praise your leadership ability.

It is difficult to assess whether you are a good leader or not. A good way to know whether you are a good leader or not is when you hear others talk about you this way, or through a 360-degree feedback / survey.

Your Target Goal (YTG): _____

Your Outrageous Goal: _____

Timeline to complete YTG: [ ] This Year [ ] 3 Years [ ] 10 Years [ ] Lifetime

Goal # 57 – Be an Expert in Something

Reason for this Goal: An expert is someone who has extensive experience and education in a particular field or subject. By becoming an expert in something, your employer or business will value you, and this will improve your chances for success and advancement in your career or business. As an employee, you have a greater chance of being rewarded with promotions and long-term employment. As a business, customers will seek you out.

Becoming an expert requires high dedication to learning, and considerable practical experience. The more specialized your area of expertise, generally the higher your income potential. Examples of areas in which you could become an expert:

* Understanding one of your products better than anyone else
* Understanding a specific disease or area of health
* Being able to repair a specific type of equipment or machine
* Using or developing a particular software or application
* Using Microsoft applications, like Excel or Word
* Understanding social media within your industry

When you really invest serious time into your field, and develop so much expertise that you standout, people won't be able to ignore you. You will create opportunities for yourself and will quite likely be viewed so positively that you will naturally develop passion towards your chosen field.

Suggested Goal(s):   I will work to become an expert in _____.

Your Outrageous Goal: I will be an expert in all areas of my profession.
At the company I work for, we call people *Subject Matter Experts* (SME), and we recognize people within our different departments as such for the areas they are highly competent in. People who are SMEs in many areas are extra valuable to our company.

Your Target Goal (YTG): _____

Your Outrageous Goal: _____

Timeline to complete YTG: [ ] This Year [ ] 3 Years [ ] 10 Years [ ] Lifetime

Goal # 58 – Become an Authority

Reason for this Goal: As the next step after becoming an *expert,* become an *authority*. The difference between an authority and an expert is that an authority is recognized and branded within their industry. The reason you want to become an authority, and not just an expert, is that because of your reputation as an authority, you will be more highly sought after and more valued. Your income will soar.

The best ways to become an authority include:

- Writing a book and becoming a published author
- Presenting at conferences within your industry
- Developing an internet presence through a website and social media
- Associating with other authorities in your industry
- Publishing newsletters or periodicals

The financial incentives to becoming an authority are significant with the difference between making a living and being truly wealthy. Some people who are authorities don't have as much knowledge as others considered true experts. It's the branding and reputation that makes you an authority. If you have set a goal to become an expert (Goal # 57), you should take it one step further to really accelerate your life and become an authority.

Suggested Goal(s): Become an authority as a _____.

Your Outrageous Goal: Be a highly sought-after authority within your industry.

To get started, there are many authorities in the publishing and self-help business who have made it very easy for you to write and publish your own book.

Your Target Goal (YTG): _____

Your Outrageous Goal: _____

Timeline to complete YTG: [ ] This Year [ ] 3 Years [ ] 10 Years [ ] Lifetime

Goal # 59 – Be Your Own Boss

Reason for this Goal: Being in a position where you have the authority to be your own boss is something that many people dream of. Having control and decision making in your career leads to success for so many people. Freedom, earnings potential, and creating a legacy are all key factors. There are various ways in which you can view yourself as your own boss:

- Starting your own business
- Taking over and buying an existing business
- Being promoted to the CEO or president of a company
- Being promoted to a senior role in a company, where you have the autonomy to run your business area with minimal oversight

While starting your own business could be viewed as the ultimate freedom, it is not for everyone and needs to be carefully considered. It will take great discipline to live your *100 Life Goals* while also running your own business. It may be that you are best in starting a *side-business* while employed in a career. There are a wide range of reasons for when you should start your own business or be your own boss:

- Following your entrepreneurial instincts early in your career
- Once you've developed significant expertise in your field
- When you're promoted to a senior position where you're essentially your own boss, as you're working for someone who has given you high autonomy to run your business area
- As part of a *side hustle,* in addition to holding a regular job (anytime within your working life)
- Towards the end of your career, later in life, as part of a retirement strategy and to pursue one of your passions

Suggested Goal(s): Become your own boss.

Your Outrageous Goal: Develop a multimillion dollar business.

Your Target Goal (YTG): _____

Your Outrageous Goal: _____

Timeline to complete YTG: [ ] This Year [ ] 3 Years [ ] 10 Years [ ] Lifetime

Goal # 60 – Create Multiple Income Sources

Reason for this Goal: Developing multiple sources of income is a great way to diversify and protect your financial health. There has never been a better time in history, due to today's technological marvels and internet advancements, to do so. With multiple sources of income, should one source end, you will have other sources already established. You can generate passive sources of income that aren't directly tied to each hour of work you get paid for, as in a traditional job.

Examples of multiple income sources include:

- Employment income (salary) from your primary job
- Income from a secondary job or side business
- Rental income from real estate
- Commissions from selling
- Buying and reselling for a profit or capital gain
- Income from a multi-level marketing business
- Interest income from investments
- Royalty income from letting others use your products, ideas, or processes (e.g., books, songs, or products)

There are very few individuals who ever become millionaires through employment income alone. The vast majority have multiple sources. Decide on what makes the most sense for you.

Suggested Goal(s): Develop a second source of non-salaried income.

Your Outrageous Goal: Develop at least 5 sources of income.

We recently just made an investment with a local real estate developer to purchase a hotel suite in a major restoration project. The investment allows us to share in the profits of a hotel and all the income that is generated through the running of this hotel. While some may consider this a risky investment, there is the promise of quarterly and annual payments, which could represent a good, additional source of income for our family. It's also a *hard asset* we can stay in while enjoying an investor experience and owning a significant piece of real estate.

As I write this book, it is possible that I will seek to develop a side business in support of this, through the site www.100GoalsClub.com. There are numerous possibilities in developing income from such an internet-based business, including:

- Cost per click (i.e. Google AdSense)
- Banner graphics
- Affiliate partnership
- Sponsored posts
- Annual memberships
- Selling of products
- Corporate consulting
- Personal consulting

I have some great people and sites that I follow, which may serve as my role models:

www.financialsamurai.com   A financial site developed by Sam Dogen, in 2009, for the purpose of financial education and achievement of financial independence.

www.rockstarbrokerage.com Tom and Nick Karadza, of Oakville, Ontario, have developed one of the best real estate investing clubs in Canada, and they also teach courses in entrepreneurial business.

Have fun, and brainstorm on ways you can create multiple income sources for yourself.

Your Goals:

Your Target Goal (YTG): _____

Your Outrageous Goal: _____

Timeline to complete YTG: [ ] This Year [ ] 3 Years [ ] 10 Years [ ] Lifetime

ADVENTURE GOALS

Life is an amazing adventure in itself. These next ten (10) goals are the kind of goals that you can get excited about; they are meant to inspire you to try something bold and adventurous. There are so many exciting things to do and experience in this lifetime. Think about these goals as a way to really create some unbelievable memories. My 10 goals in this section are:

- Take a family driving adventure(s)
- Go to a major theme park(s)
- Animal adventure(s)
- Go on a major camping trip(s)
- Take a land adventure(s)
- Take an air adventure(s)
- Take a water adventure(s)
- Take an underwater adventure(s)
- Create your own adventure(s)
- Climb a mountain

Adopt, modify, or change these 10 goals to make them your own. Once you've completed each of these, add more of these adventure goals. That is why there is an (s) at the end of each goal heading.

In my own life, I've had some of my own adventures, which are truly memorable:

- Wilderness camping on a small island in Algonquin park, only accessible by a series of portages, with my best friend; and then the next year, with our future wives
- Hot Air ballooning over the vineyards of Sonoma Valley, CA
- Travelling across Canada in two separate major trips (west and east)
- Skydiving on my 50th birthday, with my daughter, sister and family
- An underwater adventure, on an aquabike, in Bora Bora

- Horseback riding along a rugged coast line in Maui, Hawaii
- Ziplining through the rain forest, in Costa Rica
- Exploring the ancient civilization of Ephesus, in Turkey
- Powered hang gliding in Maui

Goal # 61 – Take a Family Driving Adventure(s)

Reason for this Goal: There is nothing like a *driving vacation*, with family, to create lasting memories. A vacation in which you drive instead of fly is also much less expensive, which is especially important in your earlier years.

Tips to planning and enjoying a driving vacation adventure:

- Visit places you've never been before.
- Search out places that are important landmarks or known tourist destinations.
- Stay in a variety of overnight accommodations (e.g., campground, hostel, motel, cottage hotel, bed and breakfast, Airbnb, inn, ranch, etc.)
- Take time to enjoy the journey. This trip is more about the journey than the final destination.
- Take the back roads for part of the trip, in favor of highways.
- Search out some great restaurants along the way.
- If travelling with younger children, play games along the route, like counting cows, horses, churches, flags, etc.

Suggested Goal(s): Plan and take a 1-week driving vacation.

Your Outrageous Goal: Drive across your entire country in a single vacation. When you ask children later in life about their most memorable times growing up, it is likely that your driving vacation(s) together will rank near the top.

In 2006 and 2007, our family drove across Canada—first, out West, to Victoria, British Colombia; and then, out East, to Newfoundland. We visited many of the locations on the Canada-Opoly board game. We traveled with Kathy's parents, Joe and Aurella, across our great country, spending real quality time together as a family, while exploring and seeing our vast country firsthand. It is a trip that we will always cherish, and one that I hope we repeat again some year, perhaps when our children have children of their own. I wrote out a complete travel journal of our entire trip, in Microsoft word, with embedded pictures, which may end up in a blog someday.

Some of the sites we've visited across Canada, as featured in the Canada-Opoly game board, include:

- Fort Louisburg
- Niagara Falls
- Chateau Frontenac
- CN Tower
- Magnetic Hill
- Big Nickel
- Royal Canadian Mint
- Lake Okanagan
- Lake Winnipeg
- Science World
- Canadian Museum of Nature
- Royal Tyrell Museum

We stayed in a wide range of accommodations, including hotels, inns, bed and breakfasts, the West Edmonton mall, and a ranch; and we even slept in our van on one occasion—when we had a crazy experience by running out of gas late one night.

Decide what driving adventure you could take, and make some great family memories you'll cherish forever.

Your Goals:

Your Target Goal (YTG): _____

Your Outrageous Goal: _____

Timeline to complete YTG: [ ] This Year [ ] 3 Years [ ] 10 Years [ ] Lifetime

Goal # 62 – Go to a Theme Park(s)

Reason for this Goal: There are incredible theme parks throughout most countries, which are designed to create excitement and thrills for children and adults of all ages. Some families make this an annual event. The adventures are *scalable*, based on your tolerance for thrills.

The Top 10 list of the most thrilling theme parks, according to the website, www.escapehere.com:

* Busch Gardens, Williamsburg USA
* Cedar Point, Sandusky, Ohio USA
* Everland, Yongin, South Korea
* Parc Asterix, Paris, France
* Universal's Islands of Adventure, Orlando, Florida USA
* Six Flags Magic Mountain, Los Angeles, USA
* Blackpool Pleasure Beach, United Kingdom
* Walt Disney World, Orlando, Florida
* Port Aventura, Spain
* Europa-Park, Germany

Suggested Goal(s): Go to _____ theme park.

Your Outrageous Goal: Go to the top 10 theme parks in the world.

Theme parks offer a variety of rides, shows, and amusement for all ages. In our area, we have Canada's Wonderland, just outside of Toronto, that is our *go-to* theme park, and definitely worth going.

Your Goals:

Your Target Goal (YTG): _____

Your Outrageous Goal: _____

Timeline to complete YTG: [ ] This Year [ ] 3 Years [ ] 10 Years [ ] Lifetime

Goal # 63 – Animal Adventure(s)

Reason for this Goal: The understanding and preservation of our animal kingdom is important. By connecting with animals, even though they may be captive, it reminds us all of the tremendous diversity of our planet and the need to protect them in the grand scheme of human evolution. On top of this, it's just amazing to see these animals up close and personal. Just watch a child's reaction. Seeing animals up close and personal can happen in many ways:

- In their natural habitat
- At a local zoo (see below)
- On a safari

The top Zoos around the world, as rated by Trip Advisor, from USA to Asia:

- Loro Parque, Puerto de la Cruz, Spain
- San Diego Zoo, California USA
- Chester Zoo, United Kingdom
- Singapore Zoo, Singapore
- Prague Zoo, Czech Republic
- St. Louis Zoo, Missouri USA
- Tiergarten Schoenbrunn – Zoo Vienna, Austria
- ZooParc de Beauval, France
- Bioparc Valencia, Spain

In terms of safaris, Africa is the most sought-after place to go. There are top rated safaris in places like Southern Africa (Zambia, Botswana, Zimbabwe, Namibia, South Africa, Mozambique, Malawi) and East Africa (Ethiopia, Kenya, Tanzania, Uganda, Rwanda, Madagascar, Mauritius).

Suggested Goal(s):   Visit the closest zoo to your home town.

Your Outrageous Goal: Take a 10-day African Safari.

Your Target Goal (YTG): _____

Your Outrageous Goal: _____

Timeline to complete YTG: [ ] This Year [ ] 3 Years [ ] 10 Years [ ] Lifetime

Goal # 64 – Go on a Camping Trip(s)

Reason for this Goal: Camping is about getting close to nature with an outdoor experience that you will never forget. There is nothing like sleeping in a tent outside and cozying up in a warm sleeping bag, falling asleep to the sounds of nature. If you are able to borrow some gear or purchase second hand gear, camping is more economical than staying in other accommodations, and the gear can be used over and over again.

Camping is something traditionally done during your younger years. Once we get spoiled by the modern luxury of a hotel, it can be hard to return to the basics of camping. Benefits of camping include:

- Being totally unplugged, without modern conveniences like electricity
- Being good for your mental health, producing good sleep while reducing overall stress levels, and improving your mood
- Being inspired by a sense of awe, watching sunsets and gazing at the stars, good for *recharging your batteries*
- Inhaling fresh air from all the trees and greenery that produce oxygen
- Bonding time with friends and family, telling stories over a camp fire while roasting marshmallows
- Getting out of the more sedentary lifestyle we are used to

The beauty of camping is that it is a return to basic activity; you enjoy physical activity with people you care about, in an environment that will make you feel alive again and connected with nature. My wife, Kathy, and our friends, Gary and Sue, experienced Algonquin Park together during our early courting days, and we created some great memories.

Suggested Goal(s):   Go on a 3-day camping trip in a national park.

Your Outrageous Goal: Go on a 10-day camping trip.

Your Target Goal (YTG): _____

Your Outrageous Goal: _____

Timeline to complete YTG: [ ] This Year [ ] 3 Years [ ] 10 Years [ ] Lifetime

Goal # 65 – Take a Land Adventure(s)

Reason for this Goal: As humans, we have been exploring our lands for tens of thousands of years. In modern times, exploring our lands has become much more interesting with the access to all the special equipment and technology. Make a goal to do something adventurous that is outside your normal experience. The types of land adventures you can consider include:

*   ATVing
*   Climbing
*   Dog sledding
*   Hiking
*   Hunting
*   Mountain biking
*   Mountaineering
*   Skiing
*   Snowmobiling
*   Spelunking (caves)
*   Ziplining

You can explore locally within your region, or while on vacation in some exotic location.

Suggested Goal(s):   I will take a _____ adventure.

Your Outrageous Goal: I will try all of the above adventures.

One my family's greatest land adventures was to set a goal to complete *44 Country Trails*, as in a local guidebook, featuring our area's best hiking trails.   This goal spanned over a decade while our children were young. We have several amazing photos documenting our hike, some with Maddie on my shoulders as she was young when we started these hikes.

Your Target Goal (YTG): _____

Your Outrageous Goal: _____

Timeline to complete YTG: [ ] This Year [ ] 3 Years [ ] 10 Years [ ] Lifetime

Goal # 66 – Take an Air Adventure(s)

Reason for this Goal: Travelling through the air is a thrill, no matter what form of travel. There are numerous options for an exciting air adventure, ranging from mild to highly exhilarating.

The types of air adventures you can consider include:

- Bungee jumping
- Flying in a small, fixed wing aircraft
- Flying in a helicopter
- Hang gliding
- Hot air ballooning
- Paragliding
- Parasailing
- Skydiving

Because flying in a commercial airplane is so common today, I haven't listed that as an option, but for some people who haven't flown before, that might be an adventure in itself.

Suggested Goal(s):   Plan and take an adventure around 1 of these activities.

Your Outrageous Goal: Try all of the above adventures.

Before you decide if one of these air adventures is for you, know that there can be a certain element of risk involved, and be comfortable with that.   While I, myself, am scared of heights at times, I have tried 4 of the above adventures and loved each and every one, especially hot air ballooning over the vineyards, with my wife, Kathy, in Santa Rosa, California.

Your Target Goal (YTG): _____

Your Outrageous Goal: _____

Timeline to complete YTG: [ ] This Year [ ] 3 Years [ ] 10 Years [ ] Lifetime

Goal # 67 – Take a Water Adventure(s)

Reason for this Goal: Activities associated with bodies of water (lakes, rivers, oceans) are some of the most fantastic things you can do. There is something special about being around water that brings a sense of tranquility and adventure at the same time.

Learning to swim, of course, is an important life skill; and anything to do with water is to be done with respect while taking the requisite precautions (i.e. life jackets). Following are some ideas for water adventures. Doing these in a special location/destination makes it more of an adventure, but they can also be done close to home, assuming you live near a source of water that supports it.

*   Canoeing, kayaking, rowing
*   Jet skiing
*   Kite surfing
*   Sail boating
*   Swimming a large body of water
*   Snorkeling in an exotic location
*   Surfing
*   Water skiing
*   White water rafting
*   Wind surfing
*   Yachting

Suggested Goal: Plan and take an adventure around 1 of these activities.

Your Outrageous Goal: Try all of these water adventures.

Your Goals:

Your Target Goal (YTG): _____

Your Outrageous Goal: _____

Timeline to complete YTG: [ ] This Year [ ] 3 Years [ ] 10 Years [ ] Lifetime

Goal # 68 – Take an Underwater Adventure(s)

Reason for this Goal: Since we've established goals in the air, on land, and on the water, it's only natural we take this one step further and set an underwater goal. There is an entirely different world underwater, which is foreign to most of us but must be experienced at some point in our life. Scientists report that 95% of the world's oceans have yet to be explored.

Some examples of underwater adventures are:

- Scuba diving
- Sea walk
- Snuba
- Submarine
- Underwater photography and videography
- Underwater scooter/aquabike
- Underwater resort or restaurant

Suggested Goal: Plan and take an adventure around 1 of these activities.

Your Outrageous Goal: Try all of these water adventures.

My most recent and memorable underwater experience was while celebrating our 25th wedding anniversary on a French Polynesian cruise, where we booked an underwater scooter adventure in Bora Bora, on what they called a 2-seater aquabike. The experience was incredible.

Your Goals:

Your Target Goal (YTG): _____

Your Outrageous Goal: _____

Timeline to complete YTG: [ ] This Year [ ] 3 Years [ ] 10 Years [ ] Lifetime

Goal # 69 – Create Your Own Adventure

Reason for this Goal: My first draft of this goal was an adventure goal, to *travel to outer space,* as the next frontier beyond earth. While I believe that, in my lifetime, this may be a realistic goal due to exponential technology and people like Elon Musk, my daughter cautioned me against establishing this as one of the *100 Lifetime Goals.* Before that, I had written of a *speed* adventure, as many like to seek speed thrills. But this may also have limited appeal. Instead, I'm leaving this adventure goal entirely open, as we all have different and unique ideas on adventure, which I may not have already written about. To stimulate some further ideas, I provide the following to provide some jump-off points for you:

- Explore the great Pyramid of Giza, or hanging gardens of Babylon, two of the top 7 wonders of the ancient world.
- Have a speed adventure on the world's fastest bullet train.
- Drive the autobahn in Germany, with no posted speed limits.
- Live in a foreign country for 1 month or 1 year.
- Backpack through Europe, staying in hostels.
- Vacation on a private island in the middle of nowhere.
- Take a float plane to a remote destination, and stay in a rustic camp or lodge.
- Explore an ancient civilization.
- Take a shuttle into outer space or to Mars (not currently possible, but just wait!).
- The opportunities are literally endless. Decide what lifetime adventure you aspire to achieve, and set a goal to achieve it.

Suggested Goal(s): Create and fulfill your own personalized adventure.

Your Outrageous Goal: Create and fulfill multiple personalized adventures.

Your Goals:

Your Target Goal (YTG): _____

Your Outrageous Goal: _____

Timeline to complete YTG: [ ] 10 Years [ ] Lifetime

Goal # 70 – Climb a Mountain

Reason for this Goal: When one thinks of goal setting, one of the more traditional true adventure goals that one thinks of is to climb a mountain. Climbing a mountain is a metaphor for reaching the pinnacle of your life.

The most famous mountain to climb is Mount Everest, in Nepal: the world's highest mountain, at 8,848 metres (29,029 feet). I wouldn't suggest climbing this unless you are prepared for the extreme risk involved. If you're not an experienced climber, like myself, and you would like to climb an *easier* mountain, there is a list of the world's easiest mountains to climb:

- Mount Fuji, Japan, 3776m (one of the most climbed in the world)
- Pikes Peak, United States, 4,302m (highest peak in the US)
- Tofana di Rozes, Italy, 3,225m
- Mount Hood, United States, 3,426m
- Breithorn, Switzerland, 4,164m (most climbed mountain in the Alps)
- Kilimanjaro, Tanzania, 5895m (Africa's highest mountain)
- Pico de Orizaba, Mexico, 5636m (highest mountain in Mexico)
- Island Peak, Nepal, 6,189m

Most of the above climbs are achievable in a 1-2 days and are intended for novice climbers.   If mountain climbing is not something that inspires you, choose something different, like walking up the stairs of one of the world's tallest buildings, like the CN Tower, in Toronto, Canada.

Suggested Goal(s):   Climb a mountain.

Your Outrageous Goal: Climb multiple mountains.

The inspiration for this goal came from the cover design for this book, where a mountain was used as a metaphor for goal achievement.

Your Target Goal (YTG): _____

Your Outrageous Goal: _____

Timeline to complete YTG: [ ] 3 Years [ ] 10 Years [ ] Lifetime

TRAVEL GOALS

Being able to travel is one of life's rewards. We live in a time where, if we are fortunate to have enough money, we can literally explore the entire world. Through travel, we can . . .

- Experience different cultures.
- See amazing architecture of buildings hundreds of years old.
- Meet people who have been raised entirely different to ourselves, yet find out we have so much in common.
- See how those less fortunate live, and we can develop more of an appreciation for how good we have it.
- Attend events and experience things not possible in our country.
- Eat different types of food that are authentic to a country.
- Experience music we've never heard before.
- And so much more . . .

My 10 Travel Goals that I've selected are:

- Take a staycation
- Travel your country
- Attend a major sporting event
- Attend a major cultural event
- Visit one of the 7 Wonders
- Enjoy an all-inclusive vacation
- Take a cruise ship vacation
- Go on an island vacation
- Experience an entertainment city
- Travel the world

Adopt, modify, or change these 10 goals to make them your own.

For many people, being able to travel extensively is one of the main goals for achieving financial wealth. Experiences, like travel, are some of life's best rewards for working hard and achieving financial success. You'll note that many of these goals overlap in that attending a major cultural event could allow you to visit an entertainment city, and accomplish a travel-the-world goal, all in one. When my family was reviewing this list together, we did the math to determine that someone in their twenties following this goal list would need to achieve one of these travel goals once every 5 years or so. We were concerned there might be too much travel, but a trip once every 5 years seems like a realistic goal to strive for, especially if travel is important to you, and you are able to achieve your financial and career goals.

Just a caution, though, that these goals will require sufficient financial means to be able to experience, and this kind of travel should never be paid through credit cards for which you can't afford to pay the full balance. You can travel economically or luxuriously, but ensure you understand when you're financially sound. Some of these goals may require a decade, or several decades, before you are ready.

Goal # 71 – Take a Staycation

Reason for this Goal: One of the opportunities that many of us miss out on is to be a tourist in our own area in which we live. Some of us live in or near a city that tourists from all over come to visit, but because it's in our own *backyard*, we don't think to visit it ourselves. Why not make a goal to visit all these places and explore them? Take a staycation. It is inexpensive from a travel perspective, and it would be an accomplishment to be knowledgeable and be proud of our local surroundings.

Explore the nearest tourist information office nearest to you. It could be in your own town or city, or within an hour radius of where you live. Make a list of all the places that are considered attractions to visit.   Examples include:

* Historic buildings
* Natural conservation areas or hiking trails
* Museums
* Royal Botanical Gardens
* Theatres
* Concert Halls or venues
* Animal sanctuaries, aquariums, zoos
* Amusement parks
* Natural wonders
* Spas or resorts

Suggested Goal(s): Visit the top 5 local attractions nearest to where you live.

Your Outrageous Goal: Visit every local attraction in your area within a 1-hour radius.

Your Goals:

Your Target Goal (YTG): _____

Your Outrageous Goal: _____

Timeline to complete YTG: [ ] This Year [ ] 3 Years [ ] 10 Years [ ] Lifetime

Goal # 72 – Travel in Your Own Country

Reason for this Goal: To build upon the prior goal of being a local tourist, it is natural to extend the same philosophy to your own country. Many of us are so excited about traveling afar, that we miss the opportunities to travel and explore our own country.

Depending upon which country you live in, this could be a simple or monumental task. In a country the size of United States or Canada, it could take an entire lifetime to explore. Start with researching and listing the top places and attractions that exist in your own country, and highlight the ones that resonate with you, which you'd like to visit within your lifetime.

Places to consider:

- Historical landmarks and buildings
- Your nation's capital
- Famous or unique buildings
- Natural wonders
- Tourist cities
- National landmarks
- National parks, forests, camping grounds
- Beaches, waterfronts, lakes, oceans

Suggested Goal(s): Travel to and explore the top 10 attractions or places in your own country.

Your Outrageous Goal: Travel to and explore your entire country.

Your Goals:

Your Target Goal (YTG): _____

Your Outrageous Goal: _____

Timeline to complete YTG: [ ] This Year [ ] 3 Years [ ] 10 Years [ ] Lifetime

Goal # 73 – Attend a Major Sporting Event

Reason for this Goal: Some of the greatest events are staged around major sports. With the energy and excitement of a major sporting event, decide you'll attend one of the major games associated with your sport of choice, and make a major event out of it, travelling out of town and getting caught up in the excitement. Of course, it's much more exciting if your local team or someone you know is competing for the championships.

The following is a list of some of the major sporting events of all time:

- Calgary Stampede (rodeo) – Canada
- Daytona 500 (motor sport) – USA
- FIFA World Cup (soccer) – Host Country
- The Grand National (equestrian steeplechase) – England
- The Masters (golf) – USA
- National Basketball Association Finals – USA
- Olympics, summer or winter (multiple sports) – Host Country
- Stanley Cup (hockey) – USA or Canada
- Super Bowl (NFL) – USA
- Tour De France (cycling) – France
- Wimbledon (tennis) – England
- Winter X Games (extreme sports) – USA
- World Series (baseball) – USA or Canada

There are numerous other major sporting events throughout the world. Choose something that resonates with you, or that of one of your friends or family.

Suggested Goal(s):   Attend one of the above major sporting events.

Your Outrageous Goal: Attend all of the above major sporting events.

Your Target Goal (YTG): _____

Your Outrageous Goal: _____

Timeline to complete YTG: [ ] This Year [ ] 3 Years [ ] 10 Years [ ] Lifetime

Goal # 74 – Attend a Major Cultural Event

Reason for this Goal: The culture of the country we live in, and that of other countries, is the foundation by which societies live. Attending major cultural events is a great way to experience life and find out how people of certain countries celebrate.

There are literally hundreds, and even thousands, of different major cultural events, which you could set a goal to attend. Pick something that aligns with one of your hobbies, loves, or passions. Following is a list of some potentials:

- Mardi Gras (New Orleans, USA) – Christian festival – January
- Rio Carnival (Brazil) – Biggest world carnival – February
- Grammy Awards (USA) – Music Awards – February
- Juno Awards (Canada) – Music Awards – March
- Academy Awards (USA) – Hollywood movie stars – February
- New Orleans Jazz Festival (Louisiana, USA) – Last weekend of April
- Cannes Film Festival (France) – Film festivals – May
- Toronto International Film Festival, TIFF (Canada) – September
- New York Fashion Week (NY, USA) – February and September
- Octoberfest (Germany) – The world's largest fair (food & beer) – October
- Running of the Bulls (Spain) – Traditional festival – Multiple events
- Bonhomme Winter Carnival (Quebec) – February

There are hundreds of major, local arts, folk, food, music, religious, and wine festivals around the world, and other cultural events. Time your travel goals to be able to attend one of these major events.

Suggested Goal(s): Attend a major cultural event.

Your Outrageous Goal: Attend 10 major cultural events.

Your Target Goal (YTG): _____

Your Outrageous Goal: _____

Timeline to complete YTG: [ ] This Year [ ] 3 Years [ ] 10 Years [ ] Lifetime

Goal # 75 – Visit One of the 7 Wonders

Reason for this Goal: There are seven (7) wonders of the world, which are tracked against both remarkable natural and man-made categories. Once you know about these, it's instinctive to want to know what they are and to see some of these throughout your lifetime.

There is some debate about what actually constitutes the true Seven Wonders of the World. Below are the accepted variations:

Seven Wonders of the Modern World

- Channel Tunnel – Longest undersea tunnel, between UK and France
- CN Tower – Tallest freestanding structure in the world, Toronto CA (1976–2007)
- Empire State Building – Tallest structure in the world, NY USA (1931–1967)
- Golden Gate Bridge – The longest suspension bridge span in the world, San Francisco USA (1937–1964)
- Itaipu Dam – The largest operating hydroelectric facility – Parana River between Brazil and Paraguay
- Delta Worlds/Zuiderzee Works – The largest hydraulic engineering project undertaken by the Netherlands during the 20th century
- Panama Canal – One of the largest and most difficult engineering projects ever undertaken, Panama (1880–1914)

Seven Natural Wonders of the World

- Aurora – Northern lights, predominantly seen from the Arctic and Antarctic regions
- Grand Canyon, Arizona USA – 277 miles long, with a depth up to 1 mile (6,093 feet)
- Great Barrier Reef – The world's largest coral reef system, located off the coast of Queensland, Australia
- Harbor of Rio de Janeiro, Guanabara Bay
- Mount Everest – The earth's highest mountain (8,844m), between China and Nepal
- Paricutin volcano, Mexico

- Victoria Falls – The world's largest waterfall, in southern Africa, on the Zambezi river, between Zambia and Zimbabwe

Wonders of the World

- Great Wall of China, China – Since 7th century BC
- Petra, Jordan – c. 100 BC
- Christ the Redeemer, Brazil – Opened October 12, 1931
- Maccu Piccu, Peru – c. AD 1450
- Chichen Itza, Mexico – c. AD 600
- Colosseum, Italy – Completed AD 80
- Taj Mahal, India – Completed c. AD 1648
- Great Pyramid of Giza, Egypt – c. 2560 BC (honorary candidate)

There are many other recognized lists and variations of these lists. Whenever you travel, check these lists and, if you find yourself travelling to an area where one of these wonders exists, make sure you go out of your way to visit in person.

Suggested Goal(s):   Visit one of these 7 wonders of the world, every decade.

Your Outrageous Goal: Visit all of these 7 wonders of the world, throughout your lifetime.

Having visited the CN Tower, the Golden Gate Bridge, and the Colosseum in Italy, so far on my travel journeys, I can attest to the lasting memory that these wonders will have on you. They are truly remarkable.

Your Goals:

Your Target Goal (YTG): _____

Your Outrageous Goal: _____

Timeline to complete YTG: [ ] This Year [ ] 3 Years [ ] 10 Years [ ] Lifetime

Goal # 76 – Enjoy an All-inclusive Vacation

Reason for this Goal: An all-inclusive vacation is a great way to vacation, especially in your early years as a young adult, when controlling the amount you spend on a vacation is important. With one fee, an all-inclusive vacation will cover the costs of your airfare, transfer between airport and resort, accommodations, food, and drinks.   It's a stress-free vacation to go somewhere and not need to worry about travelling between multiple locations and attractions, where you can relax at a beautiful oceanfront beach resort.

A list of some of the countries that feature a wide variety of all-inclusive, affordable resorts include:

- Antigua, Bahamas, Barbados
- Costa Rica, Cuba
- Dominican Republic
- Mexico
- Panama

At these all-inclusive resorts, there are a wide variety of included amenities for swimming, lounging, water sports, excursions, dining, and nightly entertainment.

Suggested Goal(s):   Take an all-inclusive vacation somewhere hot.

Your Outrageous Goal: Take an all-inclusive vacation every year.

For me, my first serious vacations were to all-inclusive resorts in the Caribbean, including Dominican Republic, Jamaica, and Cuba. Costs were affordable and the experiences memorable. I proposed to my wife, Kathy, at one of these resorts, in Cuba. I also had my first diving experience in Jamaica, after taking just a 30-minute introductory class in the resort pool (not recommended; more training required).

Your Goals:

Your Target Goal (YTG): _____

Your Outrageous Goal: _____

Timeline to complete YTG: [ ] This Year [ ] 3 Years [ ] 10 Years [ ] Lifetime

Goal # 77 – Take a Cruise Ship Vacation

Reason for this Goal: A cruise ship vacation offers a unique and excellent way to travel, especially as a family or with many people of different age groups. You can easily explore multiple destination ports in just one trip, getting to identify areas of the world that you wish to spend more time in with a return trip.

Some of the additional benefits of vacationing on a cruise ship include:

- Being on a floating resort, with a balcony overlooking the ocean, and being able to enjoy the sunrise and sunsets from the privacy of your own state-room.
- Talented entertainers, nightly, in the grand ball room
- Amazing and plentiful food, and multiple dining and food options, with excellent table service
- Daily activity schedules, with a wide variety of activities for all ages
- Being able to choose your area of the world to cruise and visit a unique port almost every day, to experience different cultures
- Not having to worry about travelling and moving your luggage as you are able to explore
- An easy way to get to know others and develop lifelong friendships with those you meet
- Activities for children and adults of all ages

Ten of the more popular cruise ship destinations, in alphabetical order, include:

- Alaska
- Australia
- Bahamas
- Baltic Sea
- Bermuda
- Caribbean
- Hawaii
- Mediterranean
- New Zealand
- South Pacific (Tahiti, Bora Bora, etc.)

Suggested Goal(s):   Book and take a cruise with your entire family.

Your Outrageous Goal: Take 10 cruises to the world's top destinations.

My wife and I only started cruising 5 years ago, and we enjoyed our first Caribbean cruise so much that we've taken cruises to Bermuda, the Mediterranean (Italy, Greece), and to the French Polynesian (Tahiti, Bora Bora) to celebrate our 25th wedding anniversary. We will be planning many more throughout our retirement years.

Your Goals:

Your Target Goal (YTG): _____

Your Outrageous Goal: _____

Timeline to complete YTG: [ ] This Year [ ] 3 Years [ ] 10 Years [ ] Lifetime

Goal # 78 – Go on an Island Vacation

Reason for this Goal: When you dream of the perfect vacation, many dream of an island in the tropics, with idyllic beaches, palm trees, and crystal clear blue waters. Fortunately, there are many dream vacations that you can take to beautiful islands where you can experience this. There is no better way to vacation then to really get away and relax.

The top 10 island vacations, as reported by Trip Advisor, include:

- Maui, Hawaii
- Santorini, Greece
- Jamaica
- Providenciales, Turks and Caicos
- Bali, Indonesia
- Majorca, Balearic Islands
- Mauritius, Africa
- Phuket, Thailand
- Bora Bora, Society Islands
- Fernando de Noronha, Brazil

Suggested Goal(s): Take an island vacation on your Xth (decade or quarter century) milestone birthday, or honeymoon.

Your Outrageous Goal: Visit the top 10 island vacations around the world.

We've been very fortunate to travel to Maui during the first decade of our marriage, and we loved it so much that we've been back many times. It has everything going for it, and it truly is a special place. Ensure you buy the book, *Maui Revealed*, to help plan your vacation and find all the *hidden gems* that the author recommends.

Your Target Goal (YTG): _____

Your Outrageous Goal: _____

Timeline to complete YTG: [ ] This Year [ ] 3 Years [ ] 10 Years [ ] Lifetime

Goal # 79 – Experience an Entertainment City

Reason for this Goal: There are many cities that have evolved into world class destinations, which cater to both residents and tourists, and provide a myriad of entertainment possibilities for a unique and memorable place to visit. Depending upon your interests, select from one of these destinations for a weekend or week getaway to immerse yourself in the best of what the city has to offer.

The top 10 most exciting cities in the world for entertainment and nightlife, according to a variety of websites that track popularity, with a mention to some of the key attractions, including some of the best rated concert venues (since I am a huge music lover):

TOP CITIES IN THE USA

- **Chicago,** Illinois (Wrigley Field, Navy Pier, Bars, Chicago Blues, Metro, Aragon Ballroom)
- **Los Angeles,** California (shows, night clubs, nightlife, celebrities, Hollywood Bowl, Greek Theatre, House of Blues)
- **Las Vegas,** Nevada (gambling, shows, music, shopping, circus)
- **Miami,** Florida (nightlife, clubs, Latin music, dancing)
- **New York City,** New York (shows, hotels, music, Broadway, restaurants, Radio City Music Hall, Beacon Theatre, Bowery Ballroom, Madison Square Garden, Brooklyn Bowl, Kings Theatre)
- **Nashville,** Tennessee (country music capital – "Music City," USA, Grand Ole Opry, The Ryman Auditorium)
- **New Orleans,** Louisiana (jazz, Mardi Gras, festivals, House of Blues)
- **Orlando,** Florida (Magic Kingdom, family entertainment, Walt Disney Concert Hall)
- **San Francisco,** California (Pier 39, Great American Music Hall, The Fillmore)
- **San Diego**, California (Balboa Theatre, Gaslamp Quarter)

TOP CITIES AROUND THE WORLD OUTSIDE THE USA

- **Amsterdam**, Netherlands
- **Barcelona**, Spain
- **Berlin**, Germany
- **Dubai**, United Arab Emirates
- **Hamburg,** Germany
- **London**, United Kingdom
- **Rio de Janeiro**, Brazil
- **Paris**, France
- **Toronto**, Canada
- **Tokyo**, Japan

Suggested Goal(s): Vacation in one of these amazing cities.

Your Outrageous Goal: Make your own top 10 list of world class cities to visit and experience them all firsthand.

One of my favourite memories, on a family trip to New York City, was dining at a famous musical restaurant where the venue employs Broadway singers as waiters and waitresses in their restaurant. They take turns singing as they stroll through the restaurant, to the dining pleasure of the patrons. Where else can you experience entertainment like this but in one of these special entertainment cities? Other passions of mine are architecture and music, so I've listed many of the great music venues in each of these cities.

Your Goals:

Your Target Goal (YTG): _____

Your Outrageous Goal: _____

Timeline to complete YTG: [ ] This Year [ ] 3 Years [ ] 10 Years [ ] Lifetime

Goal # 80 – Travel the World

Reason for this Goal: We have never lived at a better time than right now, to have the opportunity to travel the entire world and experience different cultures, people, historic land marks, natural wonders, and so much more.   While it will take serious money to travel the world, with the right planning and focus on goal achievement as taught in this book, these opportunities are a possibility for you and your family, in your lifetime.   There are also numerous books on how to travel the world on a budget, and staying in places like hostels.

The top destinations in the world to travel to, according to Trip Advisor as of 2017, and ranked in order of Travellers Choice, are:

- Bali, Indonesia
- London, United Kingdom
- Paris, France
- Rome, Italy
- New York City, United States
- Crete, Greece
- Barcelona, Spain
- Siem Reap, Cambodia
- Prague, Czech Republic
- Phuket, Thailand
- Istanbul, Turkey
- Jamaica
- Hoi An, Vietnam
- St. Petersburg, Russia
- Roatan, Honduras
- Marrakech, Morocco
- Ambergris Caye, Belize
- Rio de Janeiro, Brazil
- St. Martin/St. Maarten
- Playa del Carmen, Mexico
- Dubai, United Arab Emirates
- Grand Cayman, Cayman Islands
- Kathmandu, Nepal
- Bora Bora, French Polynesia
- Cusco, Peru

About 20 years ago, I was in a local craft store, where I made an impulse purchase of a *stamp*, in which the top cities in the world were listed, with unique colored fonts. We've made it a mission (and a bit of a game) to visit all of the locations on this stamp. The stamp locations are as follows:

- *Rome
- *Paris
- *London
- *New York
- Amsterdam
- *Tokyo
- Cairo
- *Chicago
- *Boston
- *Hong Kong
- *Los Angeles
- *Athens
- Prague
- Venice
- *Madrid
- Dublin
- *Barcelona
- *Washington DC
- Seattle
- Miami
- Rio De Janeiro
- *San Francisco
- Munich
- Sydney
- *Maui
- *Moscow
- Vienna
- Jerusalem
- Honolulu
- Florence
- *Montreal

At the time of this writing, the asterisked items are all the places that we've traveled so far. Australia (Sydney) has been on our dream vacation list for many years, and it is a place we will likely go to celebrate a milestone anniversary.

Suggested Goal(s):   Visit one top world destination every 10 years.

Your Outrageous Goal: Visit all 25 top locations in the world, as ranked by Trip Advisor.

Your Goals:

Your Target Goal (YTG): _____

Your Outrageous Goal: _____

Timeline to complete YTG: [ ] This Year [ ] 3 Years [ ] 10 Years [ ] Lifetime

LIFESTYLE GOALS

One of the great goals of life is to develop and live a great lifestyle. Lifestyle can mean so many different things to each of us. Lifestyle, to me, is about the manner in which we live, from the type of house we live in to the type of experiences we enjoy. In this book, my 10 goals related to lifestyle are:

- Eat at great restaurants.
- Declutter your life.
- Take weekend getaways.
- Buy high quality stuff.
- Buy your first house.
- Experience life.
- Own or have access to a vacation property.
- Pay others to do chores.
- Drive your dream car.
- Live in your dream house.

Lifestyle is one of the great rewards of life for developing financial wealth. But you can still cultivate a good lifestyle on a modest income. Travel is considered part of your lifestyle goals, for which the 10 travel goals are an integral part of lifestyle. Some of us are content with a simple lifestyle. Some of us aspire to live a grand lifestyle. Some of us go way overboard and try to live a lifestyle way beyond our means to impress our neighbours and our co-workers. It is so easy to develop that mentality as we are constantly bombarded with advertising and messaging about all the finer things in life that we should buy (fancy houses as seen on HGTV, cars as advertised in magazines, fancy clothes seen in magazines and in shopping malls, etc.). It's important to develop a realistic and healthy attitude towards all of this so that you are not living to *keep up with the Joneses*, which is an expression about buying stuff to impress your neighbours.

An important message is to live the best lifestyle you can, or aspire to, but within your *means*. If you aspire to a great lifestyle, use this book to help record what that means for you, and work on your personal development, financial, and career goals to increase your wealth to support it.

Adopt, modify, or change these 10 goals to make them your own.

Goal # 81 – Eat at Good Restaurants

Reason for this Goal: Eating at good restaurants is one of the pleasures of life. If you live in an urban area, there are so many wonderful restaurants where you can experience foods and cultures from around the world, with excellent service and inspiring ambiance and atmosphere.

Why not be adventurous and find favourite new restaurants by trying new types of food?

*   Buffet, Casual, Destination, Pub, Fast Food, Pizza
*   Fine Dining
*   Ethnic:
    [ ] Caribbean, [ ] Chinese,   [ ] French, [ ] German, [ ] Greek, [ ] Hawaiian, [ ] Indian, [ ] Italian, [ ] Japanese, [ ] Mediterranean, [ ] Mexican, [ ] Thai
*   Teppanyaki-style
*   And much more!

Have some fun doing this! It's a great way to spend time with friends or family, enjoying a good meal at a top restaurant, without cooking it yourself or cleaning up after yourself.

Suggested Goal(s):   Dine out at a good restaurant once a month.

Your Outrageous Goal: Develop a favourite restaurant for each of these categories and types of restaurants, and dine out once/week.
My wife happens to work at the top restaurant in my home town city, with a 30-year legacy of serving excellent food in a restaurant with great service and ambience. We eat there often.   We also make the habit of dining out frequently on our weekly date night (reference Goal # 24), trying out restaurants in our area.

Your Target Goal (YTG): _____

Your Outrageous Goal: _____

Timeline to complete YTG: [ ] This Year [ ] 3 Years [ ] 10 Years [ ] Lifetime

Goal # 82 – Declutter Your Life (Habit)

Reason for this Goal: Wherever you live now, or aspire to live in the future, decide that you will live in a house that is clutter-free.   When your living space is full of extra *clutter,* it can be emotionally draining and lead to decisions to not want to invite friends and family into your living space, which is counterproductive to the desire to develop great relationships with your friends and family.   It may lead to negativity about your overall living space, and a feeling that you're not living a good lifestyle.

Examples of things you can do to declutter your life:

* Think consciously about all of your material possessions you currently own, and what you should purge if it hasn't been used, and you're unlikely to use it in the future.
* Every time you receive or bring a new piece of clothing into your closet, give away one other piece.
* Avoid purchasing *knick-knacks* that lead to clutter in the first place.
* Hire an organizational consultant to get your house in order.
* Purchase quality over quantity (see Goal 84).
* emember that less is more.

Suggested Goal(s):   Declutter your living space.

Your Outrageous Goal: Keep your living spaces decluttered for the rest of your life.

Anyone who has or has had children know that the complexities of living in a clutter-free house goes up significantly with children.   Find places for your children's stuff, and develop rules for keeping the house tidy at an early age.

Your Target Goal (YTG): _____

Your Outrageous Goal: _____

Timeline to complete YTG: [ ] This Year [ ] 3 Years [ ] 10 Years [ ] Lifetime

Goal # 83 – Take Weekend Getaways

Reason for this Goal: Weekend getaways allow you to leave the daily grind and spend some time with cherished family or friends. Some of you live within an hour of local towns or cities, with local bed and breakfasts or hotels worthy of getting away and enjoying a weekend (even if just one night) and a nice dinner.

Some ideas to consider for your weekend getaway:

- A local bed and breakfast
- A big city getaway to your nearest city, to experience city life
- A local, charming town/community
- A small country inn
- Camping or RVing
- A great hotel with amenities

Suggested Goal(s): Take 2 weekend getaways a year.

Your Outrageous Goal: Take a weekend getaway, once every 3 months (each season), for life.

In our case, we live just 45 minutes away from one of the most charming towns in all of Canada: Niagara on the Lake. We make a point of getting there at least once a year for our couples' getaway; usually around our anniversary, Christmas, or one of our birthdays. We also have done the same thing with our children, to Niagara Falls, just a 1-hour drive away. It always feels like pressing the reset button on our lives when we take some time to get away, and it doesn't involve a flight or expensive vacation.

Your Target Goal (YTG): _____

Your Outrageous Goal: _____

Timeline to complete YTG: [ ] This Year [ ] 3 Years [ ] 10 Years [ ] Lifetime

Goal # 84 – Buy Quality Stuff (Habit)

Reason for this Goal: We live in a world where much of what is produced is of low quality. When you buy high quality stuff, not only does it work and make you feel better to own it, it will also last longer and be less expensive in the long run because you won't need to replace it as often. Examples of how this could apply to your life:

- Own half the number of really good clothes, whether you're talking about shirts, skirts, or shoes.
- Buy furniture made from solid wood vs. furniture you assemble yourself.
- Buy quality plumbing fixtures for your home as they need replacing.
- Own one really good watch instead of several average watches.
- Buy one great quality outdoor patio set that will last 20 or more years, versus a set you will replace after 3–5 years.

The list is endless and applies to all your purchases.

Suggested Goal(s): Develop the habit of buying quality stuff.

Your Outrageous Goal: Develop the habit of buying quality stuff, and maintain this habit for life.

Research your purchases before making them, to make the best decisions. If you can, buy quality stuff that is made locally.

I have had an annual membership to consumer reports for many years and find it helpful to see what research has been done on a product or item before I make my final decision.

Your Target Goal (YTG): _____

Your Outrageous Goal: _____

Timeline to complete YTG: [ ] This Year [ ] 3 Years [ ] 10 Years [ ] Lifetime

Goal # 85 – Buy Your First House

Reason for this Goal: The dream of many people is to one day own their own house. Depending upon your circumstances (or what you make of them), owning your own home is a perfectly reasonable goal to strive for. Not only will it give you a sense of ownership of what will likely be the most important asset in your life, it is a great way to build up your financial net worth as you pay down your mortgage and eventually own the house outright.

Reasons to own your house include:

- Personal pride of being able to look after your own house, not your landlord's
- A financial asset that will grow in value over time and develop into a retirement *nest egg* someday when you downsize
- You'll have full control over the design and renovation decisions
- You'll learn how to maintain and improve your house, instead of leaving that to your landlord
- You'll have an asset that you can borrow against, as your equity portion increases in value as your mortgage debt is paid down—your house appreciates (This is a big advantage.).

Suggested Goal(s): Buy your first house.

Your Outrageous Goal: Buy multiple houses (see Goal 46).

Owning your own house does require that you get approved for a mortgage, which typically requires a substantial deposit, a good income, and a good credit rating, all of which are possible. I purchased my first house at age 26, after graduating from college (DeVry Institute of Technology) and having started my career in sales and marketing as a Bid and Proposal Coordinator, with a steady income.

Your Target Goal (YTG): _____

Your Outrageous Goal: _____

Timeline to complete YTG: [ ] This Year [ ] 3 Years [ ] 10 Years [ ] Lifetime

Goal # 86 – Experience Life

Reason for this Goal: There are literally hundreds and thousands of different experiences that one could enjoy in a lifetime. One of the dangers of being too rigid on goal achievement is missing out on other opportunities to experience things that aren't stated goals. This goal is written so that in developing your lifestyle, you know it's okay to say yes, and I encourage you to be spontaneous and open to other opportunities to experience life. A favourite quote I read, by my early mentor, the legendary Jim Rohn, talks about saying yes to every new experience that comes your way.

Examples of times to be spontaneous and say yes to new experiences on a regular basis include:

* Your son or daughter asks you to go with them to a special event
* One of your friends asks you to go to a local event that you would normally say no to
* You receive a lunch invitation from a colleague to try out a new restaurant
* You see an advertisement in your local newspaper for a community event that interests you, but it's easy to pass on
* Any experience that comes your way that is something you haven't done before but peaks your curiosity in some way
* Any event that your grandchild is attending, and you could attend too

The key is not to get so caught up in yourself that you're not open to trying new things and broadening your life experience. Avoid falling into a rut. You never know when one of these new experiences could turn into a new passion or hobby (see section in this book on Hobbies and Passions).

Suggested Goal(s): Take advantage of opportunities for new experiences.

Your Outrageous Goal: Say yes to every new experience.

Your Target Goal (YTG): _____

Your Outrageous Goal: _____

Timeline to complete YTG: [ ] This Year [ ] 3 Years [ ] 10 Years [ ] Lifetime

Goal # 87 – Own or Have Access to a Vacation Property

Reason for this Goal: No matter how nice a home or place you live, some of us just need a place to get away. Having access to a vacation property, either one that you own, your parents own, or one that your friends own, is a great way to get out of the daily grind and get some time away. This place needs to be at least 30 minutes to 6 hours away (by car), which you can frequent, preferably without taking a flight, unless you have enough wealth that a flight is not a deterrent. Options for having access to a vacation property (where you own it or someone else does, who likes you) include:

- A cottage in the woods or on a lake
- A villa in a foreign country
- A trailer in a trailer park
- A getaway house in a private, natural setting in the woods
- A beach house on the ocean
- A recreational vehicle you can drive or leave parked at a camping site

Suggested Goal(s): Own or have access to a vacation property.
Your Outrageous Goal: Have 4 vacation properties, one for each season.

Our first vacation property was a cottage that my grandfather owned, near Buckhorn, Ontario, and we enjoyed many family getaways. Our second was a park model trailer that we co-purchased with our best friends at Sherkston Shores resort on Lake Erie, a camp ground with a wide variety of amenities that included a water park, a swim quarry, and a drive-on beach for cars and golf carts. We then sold, and purchased, in 2007, our own lake front cottage property, with two separate buildings, one of which we rent in the summers.

A word of caution: owning a cottage can be a lot of additional work with maintenance and upkeep. But when you're at your vacation property, it doesn't feel as much like work, as long as you take time to enjoy it.

Your Target Goal (YTG): _____
Your Outrageous Goal: _____
Timeline to complete YTG: [ ] This Year [ ] 3 Years [ ] 10 Years [ ] Lifetime

Goal # 88 – Pay Others to Do "Chores"

Reason for this Goal: As you work to develop and improve your lifestyle, what if you could pay someone to do all the things that you don't like doing. Consider the value of your time as you grow you career and aspire to the point that you pay people to do the work you don't enjoy. This will give you more time to do the things you love, and to focus on your life goals. Examples of chores that you should aspire to paying others to do, as part of your lifestyle plan:

- Cleaning your house or residence
- Fixing your plumbing or leaky faucets
- Maintaining your yard (grass cutting and landscaping)
- Cleaning your exterior windows, eavestroughs, and siding
- Building a deck
- Cleaning your automobile
- Doing your taxes
- Doing your *handyman* work around the house

Suggested Goal(s): Hire a cleaner and handy man for your house.

Your Outrageous Goal: Hire others to do all the things on your chores list.

It's only now that I'm well into my fifties that I've realized it's okay to pay people to do these types of chores. We've only in the past year hired a professional cleaner to clean our own house on a regular schedule. We are paying professionals to do work (like building a deck) that I once would have done— which a professional will build better, and it will last longer. I did my own taxes for many years and realized that hiring a professional was in my best interest to avoid mistakes I made previously. Working on high ladders to clean eaves troughs, or working on a roof, can be a dangerous task for the average homeowner, yet many attempt this work themselves. Pay someone who does this for a living, as part of your lifestyle plan.

Your Target Goal (YTG): _____

Your Outrageous Goal: _____

Timeline to complete YTG: [ ] This Year [ ] 3 Years [ ] 10 Years [ ] Lifetime

Goal # 89 – Drive Your Dream Car

Reason for this Goal: Some of us have a fascination with the automobile and dream about one day driving our dream car. At the time of writing this book, the majority of people own their own cars; however, it is foreseeable in the next 10 years that there will be a shift to autonomous cars, which people don't own but share. Regardless, the fascination with being able to drive a dream car will never vanish. There is something special about the dream of owning a sporty car, and driving with the windows down on a sunny day, with an open roof and the music playing.

For some, it is their dream to drive or own one of the following vehicles:

- A luxury, 4-door sedan
- A 2-door sports coupe convertible
- A vintage car
- A pick-up truck
- A 4 x 4 Jeep
- A sport utility vehicle (SUV)
- An electric, self-driving vehicle

The premium automobile brands that are valued most highly, tend to be the foreign vehicles manufactured in countries like Germany and Japan, although all automobile manufacturers produce sought-after vehicles, including US car companies. Note that this goal doesn't necessarily say that you need to *own* your dream vehicle; you could just *drive* it. The cost of owning your dream vehicle may be too much for you. There are companies that allow you to rent common dream cars and take them around a test track, or take them out for a day.

Suggested Goal(s): Choose your dream car and own it someday.

Your Outrageous Goal: Own or drive several dream cars.

My dream car, when I was in my late twenties, was a Mercedes 500SL 2-door sports coupe convertible, a car that is well out of reach of the average person. It was actually written down as one of my original 100 goals, written at the age of 30. At the time of writing this book, I have not purchased my dream car. As I've evolved over the past 25 years, my taste in automobiles has changed, and I'm now more inspired by other automobile manufacturers. But that could change again too. One thing is for sure, I do plan on driving (owning) my dream car someday, when the time is right financially, even if it is a used vehicle.

One thing I do not want to encourage is purchasing your dream car before you are financially ready to do so, which is the mistake of many young people. As a general rule of thumb, you should only purchase a vehicle that is valued at no more than 10-20% your gross annual income, or 5-10% of your overall net worth. Reference a great website that I've been following for the last couple of years, for detailed rationale on this:

https://www.financialsamurai.com/the-110th-rule-for-car-buying-everyone-must-follow/

It's also a general mistake for you to buy expensive items for status reasons. Vehicles are depreciating assets. Some of the most successful people drive modest vehicles. The purpose of this goal is to figure out what would make you really happy to own or drive, and then make it happen, within your lifetime.

Your Goals:

Your Target Goal (YTG): _____

Your Outrageous Goal: _____

Timeline to complete YTG: [ ] This Year [ ] 3 Years [ ] 10 Years [ ] Lifetime

Goal # 90 – Live in Your Dream House

Reason for this Goal: Of all the things we do, the place we spend the most time is in our house (or apartment, condo, etc.). We all have our own ideas of what it would be like to live in our perfect space, inspired by the shows featured on Home and Garden TV (HGTV), and the website, HOUZZ, and all the examples on TV and in the movies of people living in amazing spaces. Given that we are talking about lifetime goals, why not decide that someday you will live in your dream house.

The features that many consider ideal when planning their dream house include:

- Open concept living space
- Gas fireplace(s)
- Spacious rooms
- Walk-in entry and bedroom closets
- Spa-like bathrooms
- Multi-media and sound throughout
- Outdoor living space with covered deck
- Main floor or upstairs laundry room
- Man cave retreat and games room area
- Ample play area space for your children/family
- Ensuite bathroom(s)
- Multi-car garage
- Backyard oasis landscaping, with entertainment deck area

Suggested Goal(s): Live in your dream house.

Your Outrageous Goal: Live in your dream house before the age of 40.

No two dream houses are alike. Your dream house may be entirely different than someone else's. It's all relative to what has been your experience growing up and living your life to date, in terms of what you're inspired to consider your dream house. In our case, my wife and I took our 1886, small heritage home (3-bedroom, 1 bathroom), and turned it into our dream home with a large renovation in 2014, adding many of the features described above. We had every aspect of our house carefully designed, and we used the services of a professional architect and interior designer to help us. While it was a considerable amount of money, we are so happy to be living in a space that we custom designed to meet all of our needs and desires. Every day, we are thankful for being able to live in our dream house. Unlike the goal above for purchasing a dream vehicle, money you put into your dream house is an appreciating asset, which you can enjoy as it appreciates over the long term.

Your Goals:

Your Target Goal (YTG): _____

Your Outrageous Goal: _____

Timeline to complete YTG: [ ] This Year [ ] 3 Years [ ] 10 Years [ ] Lifetime

GIVING BACK/LEGACY GOALS

As we live and gain wisdom and experience, many of us start thinking about what we can do to leave the world a better place for our children and our children's children. It's great to develop and live the good life as outlined in the prior 90 goals, but these next 10 goals look to something you can do to create a lasting impact—something tangible to leave your next generation—as simple as a journal of how you lived your life, or philanthropy money that you've donated to helps others in your community.

- Keep a life journal
- Make a difference in the world
- Donate to charities
- Volunteer in your community
- Trace your ancestry
- Prepare your will
- Write a book
- Document your life
- Be a philanthropist
- Leave a financial inheritance

From this list of 10 goals, read on to find out which of these goals resonate the most and inspire you to create a legacy you and your family will be remembered for and be proud of. Adopt, modify, or change these 10 goals to make them your own.

Goal # 91 – Keep a Life Journal

Reason for this Goal: Keeping a life journal is one of the best things you can do to record, in written word, things in your life that you've done, and things that you've experienced and thought throughout your life. It helps you in the present to record what it is that is important in your life, and capture ideas for the future to inspire you. Imagine, when you die, you will have a physical asset that your children and future generations will be able to read and remember you by . . . in your own physical written word, as part of your legacy.

Things that I record in my own journal, and you may consider for yours, include:

- The most significant 1 or 2 things I've accomplished each day
- The type of exercise and duration of exercise (this holds me accountable, knowing that I document it each day)
- Special events I've attended or places I've visited
- New people that I've met, with their names
- Ideas that have popped into my head that I want to look back on
- Significant expenses or purchases I've made
- Friends or family that I've spent time with
- Actions taken towards my goals
- Where we went for date night
- Gifts I've received or given on special occasions, like birthdays
- Thoughts or feelings that I wish to later reflect on

Initially, I made periodic entries into a journal whenever the mood struck me. Now it's daily. A journal holds you accountable for your life and to your goal achievement. It provides a back up to your memory to remember important things. It provides a place to record your thoughts, goals, inspirations, and ideas. It is also something that you leave behind that will be part of your legacy when you pass. There is magic in the written word.

I started keeping random journal entries, over 15 years ago, and more recently, daily entries, about 2 years ago. My memory is not the greatest, so I really appreciate having a written journal I can look back on to reflect and remember some of the key events in my life.

Suggested Goal(s):   Write daily entries into a journal for 1 year.

Your Outrageous Goal: Write daily entries into a journal for your entire life.

Your Goals:

Your Target Goal (YTG): _____

Your Outrageous Goal: _____

Timeline to complete YTG: [ ] This Year [ ] 3 Years [ ] 10 Years [ ] Lifetime

"A life worth living is a life worth recording." — Jim Rohn

Goal # 92 – Make a Difference in the World

Reason for this Goal: One of the greatest philosophies is to "leave the world a better place than when you arrived." During your epitaph, wouldn't it be amazing if people could say that you did something good that made a difference in this world.

The world is a small or big place, depending upon how you view it, due to globalization and how interconnected we all are. Below are some things that you could do that would make an impact on this world.

- Work for a company that sells products, which have a real impact
- Support an environmental cause that has far-reaching impact
- Develop a new product or service that has global impact
- Volunteer in a 3rd world country and help build a house or bring water to a community that didn't exist before
- Sponsor a child in a country that needs sponsorship
- Write a book that has a positive message

Suggested Goal(s):   Determine what it is that you will do, by which you will leave the world a better place for having lived . . . and then do it.

Your Outrageous Goal: Do something globally that has the potential to impact millions of people around the world.

I work for a global company that seeks to create a safer world by selling technology that helps find missing people, protects law enforcement, and deters illegal border crossings and terrorism, while protecting our troops abroad.

At the time of writing this book, I've been reading a book called, *Abundance . . . The Future is Better Than You Think*.   The authors are encouraging people to get involved in projects that have the potential to impact millions (and billions) of people around the world through advances in artificial intelligence, robotics, nanomaterials, synthetic biology, and other exponentially growing technologies. Reading this book may change your view on our future world.

In writing and promoting this book, it is my hope that I will inspire you to write down your goals and live a more fulfilling life so that you will achieve goals that you wouldn't have otherwise achieved. Find a cause or mission that has far-reaching impacts on our world and our planet.

Your Goals:

Your Target Goal (YTG): _____

Your Outrageous Goal: _____

Timeline to complete YTG: [ ] This Year [ ] 3 Years [ ] 10 Years [ ] Lifetime

Goal # 93 – Donate to Charities

Reason for this Goal: Helping others less fortunate than ourselves is a great way to live. There are millions, and perhaps billions, of people in this world who are living life without what we consider to be essential necessities for living a good life. Often, we forget about the people that need help in our very own community. Some of the top charitable organizations that you can support include:

- United Nations Children's Fund (UNICEF) – helping defend the rights of children across 190 countries
- Human Rights Watch – Reporting on human rights conditions, in some 90 countries, to press for changes in policy and practice that promote human rights and justice around the world
- Doctors Without Borders – Medical aid where it is needed most
- American Red Cross – Responding to people in crisis, from small house fires to multi-state natural disasters throughout the US
- Greenpeace – An independent, global campaigning organization that acts to change attitudes and behaviour, to protect and conserve the environment (climate change, forests, oceans)
- United Way – Improving lives by mobilizing the caring power of communities around the world to advance the common good
- World Vision – A global relief, development, and advocacy organization, partnering with children, families, and their communities to reach their full potential by tacking the causes of poverty and injustice
- Make A Wish – To grant the wish of every child diagnosed with a critical illness
- And hundreds more organizations supporting everything from health research to religious donations, to funding to support the homeless.

Donating money is a very personal decision, with no right or wrong amount. The average amount donated is reported to be in the range of 3% to 5% of one's net or gross income.

Suggested Goal(s): Donate 3% of your income, annually, to the charities of your choice.

Your Outrageous Goal: Donate 10% or more of your income, annually, to the charities of your choice.

Many live in an affluent community; however, there are neighbourhoods and people who struggle amongst us, who are not visible to many and go unnoticed. Through our support of organizations like United Way, there are numerous local community groups that get supported financially to make a real difference. One of the organizations that we continue to support through workplace donations (payroll deduction) is United Way, as they support so many different local community groups in need.

Your Goals:

Your Target Goal (YTG): _____

Your Outrageous Goal: _____

Timeline to complete YTG: [ ] This Year [ ] 3 Years [ ] 10 Years [ ] Lifetime

Goal # 94 – Volunteer in Your Community

Reason for this Goal: In your own community, there are numerous volunteering opportunities in which you can support the needs of people and projects, to improve and benefit the lives of others in need. Helping the needs of those in your own community directly impacts and improves those around you, and has intrinsic rewards in helping others.

Examples of volunteering opportunities that may exist in your community include:

- Community clean-up days to pick-up litter and clean up neighbourhoods
- Helping out a homeless shelter
- Delivering *welcome* packages to newcomers who move into the community from another country
- Volunteering at your church or religious organization
- Preparing or cooking meals at a soup kitchen, or in support of a holiday event, like Thanksgiving or Christmas
- Fundraising for a charitable health organization
- Helping to build a house for Habitat for Humanity
- Festivals and events volunteer opportunities in your community
- Volunteering at a senior's center or retirement home
- Being a Big Brother or Big Sister to mentor a young child
- And 100s of other organizations looking for your volunteer support

Search on-line for volunteer opportunities in your local area.

Suggested Goal(s): Be an active volunteer with an organization of your choice for 1 year.

Your Outrageous Goal: Be an active volunteer with 1 or more organizations of your choice for a lifetime.

Your Target Goal (YTG): _____

Your Outrageous Goal: _____

Timeline to complete YTG: [ ] This Year [ ] 3 Years [ ] 10 Years [ ] Lifetime

Goal # 95 – Trace Your Ancestry

Reason for this Goal: We all have a life story that precedes us, which is part of our legacy and who we are, but many of us don't know what that is. With the advent of the internet, DNA testing, and on-line information that has been compiled about people, it is now possible to extensively research and find out more about our roots and our prior generations of family. In connecting with our past, it can give us a greater sense of who we are.

Following are some methods in how to trace your ancestry:

- Do all your ground work before searching on-line, starting with yourself and working back through all your records.
- Interview your parents and grandparents, and take notes.
- Share your work with your family when they drop by for a visit.
- Look for documents and records, such as death certificates, marriage records, census records, immigration records, church records, court records, and public libraries.
- Talk to family members at family reunions, and find out who else may be interested or who has already started doing this.
- Use the services of one of the hundreds of online websites, such as Ancestry.com, with extensive records, including census records.

It is important to stay organized and develop methods of storing and archiving all the information that you will come across. It's likely you will need a combination of computer files, filing cabinet folders, and 3-ring binders to organize all your information. There are even professional websites available, such as www.fileyourpapers.com, to help with this very process.

Suggested Goal(s):   Document your ancestry.

Your Outrageous Goal: Write a book about your ancestry.

Your Target Goal (YTG): _____

Your Outrageous Goal: _____

Timeline to complete YTG: [ ] 3 Years [ ] 10 Years [ ] Lifetime

Goal # 96 – Prepare Your Will

Reason for this Goal: Having a will communicates and documents your intentions on what will happen to your estate when you die. Without a will, it is left up to the government and others as to what will happen. It may not be what you would have wanted to happen. Having a well written will ensures that your estate (your assets) you have worked so hard to achieve will be dispersed in the manner you desire, and that your health care directives are carried out.   It will give you peace of mind knowing that your family knows you thought of them and planned for their future. The following are some things that need to be considered with will preparation:

• Your will needs an executor: someone accountable to ensure that the will is executed according to your plan.
• Your will needs two powers of attorney: one to deal with your finances and one to look after your health care needs. These two people act on your behalf if you are still alive but incapable of making your own decisions, due to serious health issues.
• Your will needs a guardian appointed if you have children under the age of 18, so that someone you trust makes the important decisions instead of someone appointed by the courts.
• You should consider writing a memorandum and/or a letter of wishes to document things of sentimental value to be passed down, which could change over time, so it can be more easily updated (i.e. special jewelry, artwork, furniture, or musical instruments).
• Your will needs to be updated as you age and your family situation changes, especially after major life changes such as the birth of a child or a divorce, or significant change or additions to your assets.

Suggested Goal(s):   Have a will prepared, and keep the original in a safe.

Your Outrageous Goal: Update your will every 3 years.

Your Target Goal (YTG): _____

Your Outrageous Goal: _____

Timeline to complete YTG: [ ] This Year [ ] 3 Years [ ] 10 Years [ ] Lifetime

Goal # 97 – Write a Book

Reason for this Goal: It is my belief that everyone has at least one book in them. Life is an amazing adventure in which you will develop expertise, knowledge, and experience, in a way that is truly unique to you. Why not document it in a book that will form a part of your legacy, to be passed down to future generations. Beyond that, a book will help develop your career or help recognize you as an authority in a specific area, which will lead to more life experience.

There are many organizations and publishers today who have set up systems and processes that make it very easy for someone, who has never before written a book, to do so at a reasonable cost. For me, it was Raymond Aaron's 10–10–10 publishing program that has resulted in this book you are reading right now. Following are some potential topics on which you could write your very own book:

- The Life of "_____" (a family history)
- The Book of "_____" (insert your expertise or passion here)
- "X" steps to achieving "_____" (write about an area of expertise you've developed and can help others with)
- A fiction novel, telling a story about something that you are inspired to write about
- Life lessons on how "_____" (insert your choice of topic here)

Suggested Goal(s): Write a book.

Your Outrageous Goal: Write multiple books.

It was one of my original 100 goals, written at the age of 30, to write a book. The reason I wanted to write a book was to create something that would be part of my family's legacy, in regard to *Publish an inspirational tape(s)/book to pass onto future generations*, under the category of *father (family)* goals. I'm showing my age by mentioning cassette tapes, which were the method of recording audio at the time. It is my sincere hope that this book will inspire future generations, not only in my family's lineage but throughout the world, to live a goal-oriented life and achieve more than they thought was possible.

Recently, I purchased a book from a friend of a family member who just authored and published her own book: *Explore, Transform, Flourish . . . Support and Hope for Those Who Help Others*. Gillian Stevens wrote this book about her own life experience as a secondary school guidance councillor, helping at-risk youth to overcome barriers leading to graduation. She told me it has been a transformative experience writing this book and becoming an author, something she has wanted to do for some time.

Even though you may be unsure of this goal, I encourage you to set it as one of your own personal goals. Write it, and whether you publish it or not, it could be just the thing for you to accomplish. Who knows what you'll have to write about 20 years from now! It could give your life or career a boost, and provide opportunities that will lead to greater success and life experience.

Your Goals:

Your Target Goal (YTG): _____

Your Outrageous Goal: _____

Timeline to complete YTG: [ ] This Year [ ] 3 Years [ ] 10 Years [ ] Lifetime

Goal # 98 – Document Your Life Story

Reason for this Goal: While I've written about goals to keep a journal and to write a book, these may not adequately document what you'd like to say and record about your life, documented for your children, your grandchildren, and further down the generational line.   Genealogy is becoming one of the most popular hobbies.   There have never been more forms to document your life story, and I suspect that with the coming prevalence of Artificial Intelligence (AI), your entire life may be documented automatically for you.

Things that are worthy of documenting about your life experiences include:

* The major milestones of your life (dates, events, etc.)
* The things in life that inspire you
* The things in life that bother you
* Your goals
* Your favourite memories and stories
* Your best friends
* The highlights of your career and favourite people
* What you consider your major achievements and successes
* Your favourite music (bands, songs, lyrics, etc.)
* Your favourite places
* Your favourite restaurants
* Your regrets
* Things that you'd like others to know about you

Knowing that someday you will document your life may inspire you to live your best life.   Use a combination of the written word, photographs, and video content.

Suggested Goal(s):   Document your life story.

Your Outrageous Goal: Write an autobiography about your life.

Your Target Goal (YTG): _____

Your Outrageous Goal: _____

Timeline to complete YTG: [ ] This Year [ ] 3 Years [ ] 10 Years [ ] Lifetime

Goal # 99 – Be a Philanthropist

Reason for this Goal: A philanthropist is someone who seeks to promote the welfare of others, especially by the generous donation of money (and/or time) to good causes to make other people's lives better. One of the great reasons to achieve the financial goals suggested in this book is so that you will be in a position throughout your life, particularly during the latter part of your life, to give away some of your wealth to organizations to make people's lives better.

This goal is in addition to donating to charities, which is the topic of goal # 93, and is more focused on helping distribute some of the wealth you've accumulated throughout your life, while still having money to support the next goal, to leave a financial inheritance.

Your personal reasons for being a philanthropist could include:

* A way of giving back for all the success you've achieved
* A sense of moral duty
* In support of a religious belief
* To help cure a disease
* To improve access to something for people, like education, health or care
* For political reasons, to support a political cause
* To invest in education for those combatting poverty

There are examples of high profile individuals in your community who are philanthropists, who have donated large sums of money for great causes. Sometimes they are recognized by having their name attached to a building, representing the organization they supported (e.g., in our area, the name, Michael Lee Chin, who is a Jamaican business magnate, investor, and well-known philanthropist for supporting such things as the Joseph Brant Hospital Foundation and the Royal Ontario Museum in Toronto).

There is a book written by Tracy Gary: *Inspired Philanthropy: Your Step-by-Step Guide to Creating a Giving Plan and Leaving a Legacy.* In this book, she makes the point that you don't have to be rich to be a philanthropist. She suggests that philanthropy is more about bringing your giving in line with your hopes for a better world.

Suggested Goal(s): Donate up to X% of your net worth to worthy causes during the last two decades of your life.

Your Outrageous Goal: Donate more than $_____ to worthy causes.

Your Target Goal (YTG): _____

Your Outrageous Goal: _____

Timeline to complete YTG: [ ] This Year [ ] 3 Years [ ] 10 Years [ ] Lifetime

Goal # 100 – Leave a Financial Inheritance

Reason for this Goal: Leaving a financial legacy to your children is one of the great reasons to develop a good net worth. But with this comes a responsibility to teach our children that any financial inheritance needs to be received and managed responsibly. It also should not be expected or viewed as an entitlement; it should instead be received as a *bonus* that will enhance their own financial position, at whatever time in their life it should occur.

Being able to pass along a financial inheritance to our children can benefit them in many ways:

*   Help support their own retirement plan
*   Support them in their ability to support charities of their choosing
*   Continue the philanthropy work in your honor
*   Help them help their own children with the purchase of their first home, or establish their first investment portfolio
*   Etc.

It is the goal of many parents that their children are able to develop their own financial ability to live a great life, without dependence on a financial inheritance. We live in a time where the future is uncertain, and our ability to leave a financial inheritance can leave us, as parents, with a great sense of accomplishment and reason to achieve a successful financial life.

Suggested Goal(s):   Leave a financial inheritance to each of your children.

Your Outrageous Goal: Leave a significant financial inheritance of more than $ _____ to each of your children.

Your Goals:

Your Target Goal (YTG): _____

Your Outrageous Goal: _____

Timeline to complete YTG: [ ] This Year [ ] 3 Years [ ] 10 Years [ ] Lifetime

ADDITIONAL TIPS TO ACHIEVE GOALS

Since this book is about goal setting and life design, you will likely need to step up your game to achieve the goals you are about to set. There is no better way to become a better person than to immerse yourself in the field of self-help and personal development, to improve your potential for success. Some people are born into families where these skills, principles, and habits are engrained into us . . . most of us are not, and we need to develop them throughout our life. It is my experience that these additional success principles are important to accomplishing the 100 life goals you are about to set.

Do the Top 2 or 3 Most Important Things Every Day

It is most important that you are continually progressing towards the achievement of worthwhile goals. The best way to do this is to decide, at the beginning of each day, what the 2 or 3 most important things are that you will do today that will move you forward. If you just let your day unfold without prioritizing these 2 or 3 things, you will drift. Management of your time, and putting in quality time into the things that matter, is going to be key to your successful achievement of your 100 goals. Read books on how to manage your time. It really comes down to being able to prioritize your time and ensure, every day, you are putting time into the things that matter most.

I'm currently using the Productivity Planner, produced by Intelligent Change, which was recommended to me by Tom Karadza, at Rock Star Real Estate. This planner is entirely designed to focus your most important task(s) (MIT) of the day.

Working on your most important goals, every day, is the most powerful thing!

Develop High Energy

My mentor, Raymond Aaron, is famous for saying that high energy equals high income. It's true. Think of all the most successful people in this world, and you'll see that most exhibit and have lots of energy. They walk faster, they talk faster, and they speak confidently. It's often been said of me at my long-term place of employment, that I must be taking something because of my high energy level. People naturally assume that I must be a coffee drinker, but I am not. Think about what it is you could do to improve and increase your energy level. I can tell you that some of the key contributing factors include:

- Eating well
- Exercising regularly
- Having passion and purpose in your life

There is not much that gives a lower impression of you when meeting other people than having low energy. Notice that some people walk 50–100% faster than the average person. When I know where I'm going, I want to get there as fast as I can, so that I can get whatever it is that I'm doing, done. Perhaps it's because I've worked in a fast paced, deadline driven environment, and the difference between getting something done on time, or not, are the seemingly little things, including how fast I walk. But as a cautionary note, my daughter, Karah, sometimes reminds me to stop and smell the roses, and enjoy what's in front of me!

Start observing people's energy and if the people you like to be around have low amounts or high amounts of energy. Assess your own level of energy, and ask yourself if you'd like to exhibit a higher level of energy, especially now that you know high energy can lead to higher income.

Set and Prioritize: Work on Your Goals Every Month

Once you've written your goals, it will be important to stay focused on them. One of the best ways to do that is to commit to a monthly cycle of reviewing your goals and planning what you will do in the coming month, week by week. Writing out your goals is a good thing. Reviewing them routinely is even better. Commit to printing and posting your goals where you can see them and be inspired by them. Then commit to reviewing and recommitting to them annually, either at the time of your birthday or the start of the year, for January 1st. There is power in picking these times of the year to recommit to your goals.

In planning your days, consider planning using the following method:

Life Goals - Plan your life using these 100 goals as your starting point for designing your ideal life.

Annual Goals – At the end of each year, plan ahead for the specific goals you will focus on for the year ahead. Record these in a place and review them constantly.

Monthly Goals – At the end of each month, plan your coming month while staying true to your annual goal commitment. Note that some people prefer to focus on quarterly over monthly goals. Either way, decide what works for you, and ensure you are staying true to your annual goals by retaining focus.

Weekly Goals – Focus your goals so that each week you are making meaningful progress towards your quarterly or monthly goals.

Daily Goals - This is where you select the 2 or 3 most important things to do each day that positively move you forward towards your goal completion.

Do the Opposite of What the Masses are Doing

There is a theory that exists, which says to look at what the masses are doing and do the opposite. The majority of people are followers and are on a path that does not lead to the type of success I'm writing about with this book. If you truly want to be successful, it is likely that you will need to do the opposite of what the majority of people are doing. Here are some examples of what the majority of people do (or don't do), which you may want to consider deviating from:

- Watching too much TV
- Eating out at fast food restaurants too often
- Not getting enough daily exercise
- Living in their comfort zone and being risk adverse
- Not reading books once graduated from high school or university

- Not investing at least 10% of their income

Observe what is happening with the majority of people, and decide whether they are achieving the results you want in your life. If not, try the opposite.

Take Risks (Do Things that Scare or Stretch You)

When you look back at your life's greatest moments, it is highly likely that your most memorable events and times that you recall will be when you did something outside of your comfort zone. In fact, it is quite probable that you felt some fear but did it anyway, which leads me to one my favourite expressions: *Feel the fear, but do it anyway!* Some examples from my life when I felt fear, took the action, and now recognize it as one of my top achievements, include when I . . .

- Spoke at an event, to advance my career, on *How to Write a Winning Proposal*
- Parachuted from an airplane
- Was the Master of Ceremonies at my company's Christmas party
- Bought my first house (and my second, third, and fourth)
- Drove the backside of Maui, on the drive past Hana
- Presented to 700+ real estate investors at a Rock Star Real Estate event
- Promoted this book for the first time

You get the idea. All these events involved some component of fear, but I pushed through it, and it ended up being an experience that I remember and celebrate most in my life. There are entire books written on facing your fears and doing something each day that you fear.

MY GOAL TRACK RECORD

You may be wondering about my own personal track record on achieving my personal goals and the 100 goals of this book. Fair question. It is true that I have been setting and achieving goals for well over 30 years. I've had my share of successes, disappointments, and failures. But what would life be like without this? Of the 100 goals in this book, at the time of writing this book (2018), I have achieved approximately 80% of the *target* goals in this book, and a few of the *outrageous* goals. Here is my record of achievement . . .

1 – Read (Study) Self-Help (1989 to present)
I have a library of well over 100 books, which I've read (and re-read) over the last 25 plus years, including audio courses by some of the greatest leaders in the self-help industry.

2 – Define Your Core Values (2002 – updated in 2017)
Reference Goal #2 for the core values I established in 2017 to live out the balance of my life: Integrity, Optimism, Courage, Encouragement, Knowledge ·

3 – Attend Personal Development Seminars (1993 to present)
Over the years, I've attended Improve Your Life seminars; a Master Key seminar; Real Estate Wealth Expo, with guest speaker, Tony Robbins; self-help seminars, with guest speakers, including Jim Rohn, Robin Sharma, and Brian Tracy.

4 – Develop a *Power Hour* (1993 to present)
My current power hour consists of writing and goal setting (30 minutes), exercising (20–30 minutes), and meditation (5–10 minutes).

5 – Find a Mentor (1988 to present)
My mentors include my Karate Sensei (1986-1994), Jim Rohn (1990 to 1999), Robin Sharma (2000 to present), Chris Crowley and Henry Lodge (2015 to

present), Tom and Nick Karadza (2013 to present), and Raymond Aaron (2017 to present).

6 – Learn Continuously (work in progress).

7 – Develop your Positive Attitude (1988 to present, work in progress)
I started listening to motivational speakers, and reading self-help books, when I was in my twenties. I continue to develop and improve my attitude.

8 – Develop Communication Skills (2001–2002)
I achieved the level of Competent Toast Master (CTM) after having completed a series of 10 speeches, each focused on a different aspect of speaking (speech organization, body movement, vocal dynamics, etc.). My largest speaking audience, to date, was approximately 700 people.
I have a *Future Goal* to develop an ability to tell captivating jokes/stories (one of my original 100 Goals set at age 30).

9 – Write Your Life Purpose (2017)
See this goal section for details. My most important mission is *family*, followed by *living and teaching a goal-inspired life*.

10 – FUTURE GOAL – to discover my spirituality (TBD)

11 – Eat Healthy (1970s to present)
Healthy eating has been a continuous focus throughout my life; thanks to my father, Morley Klodt, who was very health conscious throughout my entire up-bringing.

12 – Maintain Your Ideal Body Weight – Complete (+/- 15 lbs since 1991)

13 – Be Aerobically Fit (2016)
I have been working on my aerobic fitness level since 1988. I began working on cardio and HIIT 5X/week, since January 2016.

14 – Be Strong – Lift Weights (2016)
On and off, since 1990, I have been lifting weights, including through gym memberships and at home. I began weekly weight workouts at home in 2016. I can do 50+ consecutive push-ups at the age of 55 (My outrageous goal is 100.).

15 – Develop a Calm Mind (1990 to present)
I learned Tai Chi and meditation during my Karate days. I continue to meditate some mornings at the end of my power hour.

16 – FUTURE GOAL – to learn how to Prepare Healthy Meals (TBD)
My wife, Kathy, does all our cooking and food preparation, and it is at the recommendation of my family that I, too, learn how to cook healthy meals as part of my goal setting.

17 – Learn Self Defence (1986–1993)
I earned my first and second-degree Black Belt in Goju Ru Karate, training for 7 years, during my twenties.

18 – Complete an Endurance or Obstacle Course Event (2014)
I completed a Tough Mudder obstacle course, a gruelling (and muddy) event!

19 – FUTURE GOAL – to play hockey or another team sport
I have supported our children in performance level sport (Karah: nationally ranked rhythmic gymnast on Canadian national team (2010/11); Maddie: equestrian rider, ranked at the provincial and university levels).

20 – Develop a Long-Life Mindset (1963–?)
I have a goal to live healthy to the age of 100, and the mind set and expectation to go along with it. So far, so good . . . only time will tell.

21 – Choose Good Friends (done)
I have great, long-term friendships that will continue throughout my lifetime.

22 – Find Your Life Partner (1991)
I'm happily married to Kathy Klodt, for 27 years and counting . . .

23 – Treat Your Partner as a VIP – Work in progress *(ask Kathy)*

24 – Family and Weekly Date Nights (2002 to present)
Every Wednesday is family or date night, and has been for close to two decades.

25 – Learn How to Be a Good Parent (1994 to present)
Our children are now well-established young adults, pursuing professional

careers with a good foundation for life. We're still seeking to be better parents, as this is a continuous goal.

26 – Be There for Your Children (1994/1998 to present)
As parents, we were both active in all of their life events, including bedtime reading, school events, parent-teacher meetings, and years of taking them to their rhythmic gymnastics (Karah) and equestrian (Maddie) practices and competitions.

27 – Have regular Family Meetings (2004–)
We began family meetings formally and transitioned to weekly dinner nights. We had many family meetings to review the contents of this book before publishing. We plan on continuing this even though our children have grown up.

28 – Annual Family Traditions (ongoing with both sides of our family)
We have two very special families with whom we celebrate all birthdays, holidays, and special events together.

29 – Be a Good Friend (1989 to present)
My wife and I have been friends with the couple who introduced us, for more than 30 years, as well as having great friendships with many others.

30 – Be a Good Son, Daughter, Sibling (to present, work in progress)
I have strived to be a good son to my parents, Morley and Gunnell, who have supported me and my family throughout my life, and a good brother to my sister, Laura.

HOBBIES & PASSIONS (Unique Goals)

Some of my hobby goals that I've completed to date are:

31 – Started and performed with a 7-piece rhythm & blues band that was called Groove Doctors (1997–1999)

32 – Purchased a drum set and performed in a band as a drummer (2017)

33 – Restored our Gables on the Park properties (1992 to present)

34 – Developed a love for skiing with my daughter, Madison (2003 – present)

35 – Attended 10 concerts with my favourite bands (2003 – present)
One of the reasons for writing this book is to hold myself more accountable for achieving future goals. Here are my **next 5 future *Hobby & Passion* goals** that excite me:

36 – FUTURE GOAL – Start or join an amazingly talented band and perform at high profile charity events. (TBD)

37 – FUTURE GOAL – Bike around Lake Ontario (1017 Km) with my daughter, Karah, on a 10-day trip. This is a *decade* goal I set with Karah in 2003, when I turned 40, yet to be completed. (TBD)

38 – FUTURE GOAL – Learn and perform 10 guitar singalong campfire songs from memory, and do this whenever there is an opportunity (cottage parties, Christmas parties, other gatherings). (TBD)
Outrageous Goal – Write and record my own song.

39 – FUTURE GOAL – Do an amazing Christmas lights display (to music) on our 4 Gables on the Park heritage homes. (TBD)

40 – FUTURE GOAL – Interview 10 successful people about their goals and keys to success. (TBD)
Outrageous Goal – Interview 37 successful people (37 is my favourite number, based on the 37 *Decade Goals* I wrote for myself when I turned 40).

41 – Learn Personal Finances (1988 to present)
I have been reading about and applying personal finance principles for more than 30 years.

42 – Learn a Financial Tool to Manage Money (1989 to present)
I have been using excel to track our finances, and for financial applications at my work, for more than 25 years.

43 – Develop a Budget and Track Our Cash Flow (2007 to present)
I began formally tracking our cash flow in 2007.

44 – Develop a Good Credit Rating (1989 to present)
We have borrowed significant amounts of bank money to support our real
estate investing over the last 20 years (Banks won't loan without good credit.).

45 – Track and Develop Your Net Worth (2014)
Our net worth has grown at an average rate of 20% per annum for > 20 years.

46 – Invest 10% of Your Income (since 1995)
We have developed a significant portfolio in stocks and mutual funds, investing
10% of our income for the past 20+ years.

47 – Find a Good Financial Adviser/Mentor (1997–)
We have been using a financial adviser since 1997.

48 – Own Investment Real Estate (1989 to present)
We own an entire street of 4 heritage properties, known as Gables on the Park.

49 – Increase Your Income (1991 to present)
I have made excellent income growth, in both my career and with our rental real
estate income, over the past 15+ years, with income in the top 5% of
Canadians.

50 – Plan Your Retirement (2017–)
I created a detailed financial plan for our retirement (excel based) in the fall of
2017, with 3 different scenarios.

51 – Do a Career Assessment (early 2000s)
My employer had me do several self-assessments as part of career and
leadership development.

52 – Get Educated (1987–)
I am a college graduate, from DeVry Institute of Technology (Toronto), as an
Electronics Technologist.

53 – Find or Develop Your Passion (2018)
I have been *searching* for years. In 2018, I finally read the book, *Be So Good They
Can't Ignore You*, by Cal Newport, which put finding my passion into perspective.
My other passion is self help and *goals*, which this entire book is about.

54 – Join a Professional Organization (2014–2015)
I was a member of the Association for Proposal Management Professionals
(APMP), and continue to encourage my staff to join and support.

55 – Be a Good Employee (1991 – work in progress)
I have many years with good performance review ratings in the *Exceeds
Requirements* category.

56 – Be a Good Leader (2017 – work in progress)
I was responsible for leading a team of 15 Bid and Proposal staff, through a
successful transition year, when two smaller teams merged into one team,
issuing bids worth over 2 billion dollars annually. I lead daily *stand-up* meetings
and monthly team meetings with engaged employees.

57 – Be an Expert in Something (2001 to present)
I was recruited by Federated Press, in 2001, to teach a class on "How to Write a
Winning Proposal." I presented to 700+ real estate investors about furnished
rentals, in 2018.

58 – Become an Authority (2018–2019)
I authored a book—*Buy Your Neighbour's House,* a wealth building strategy for
buying real estate on your own street—as well as the writing of this book, *100
Life Goals.*

59 – Be Your Own Boss (1989 to present)
I have been a real estate investor and property manager since 1989. I am
launching the on-line business, 100GoalsClub.com, in support of this book.

60 – Create Multiple Sources of Income (1989 to present)
My sources of income have included employment income as a Bid and Proposal
Manager, tenant rental income as a real estate investor, and band income as a
bass playing musician.

61 – Take a Family Driving Adventure (2006–2007)
We drove across Canada, to Victoria, British Colombia (2006), and to
Newfoundland (2007), in a minivan with our family and my wife's parents,
visiting the locations on the game board, Canada-Opoly.

62 – Go to a Theme Park (2004)
We celebrated my parents' 50ᵗʰ wedding anniversary with a trip to Disney World, with my parents, sister, and both our families.

63 – Animal Adventures (2002–)
I have been to several zoos over the past 20 years, and the African Lion Safari (Canada). We are planning to take a safari trip to Africa someday.

64 – Go on a Camping Trip(s) (1989–1990)
I camped at Algonquin Park during a guys' portaging trip, and a guys and gals portaging trip. It was deep into the woods and only accessible by canoe.

65 – Take a Land Adventure (1999–2006)
We completed 43 of 44 country hiking trails, taking family hikes over a 6-year period, between 1999 and 2005. We were inspired by a book, entitled *44 Country Trails,* written by Katherine Jacob, and published in 1998.

66 – Take an Air Adventure (2004/2013/2018)
I went hot air ballooning in Santa Rosa, California, with my wife, Kathy.
On my 50ᵗʰ birthday, I went parachuting with my daughter, sister, and some of my family, at Burnaby Skydive. We also went *powered* hang gliding in Maui, for 45 minutes into the clouds.

67 – Take a Water Adventure (early 2000s)
My biggest water adventure was sail boating across Lake Ontario, in the middle of the night, from Youngstown, NY, to Toronto.

68 – Take an Underwater Adventure (2017)
My wife and I went on an underwater scooter adventure in Bora Bora, in a 2-seater aqua bike.

69 – FUTURE GOAL – to create my own adventure
My family and I will create our own amazing adventure.

70 – FUTURE GOAL – to climb a mountain (TBD)
I've been inspired by the initial cover design for this book, to climb a mountain.

71 – Take a staycation (1990s to present)
We make a point of attending local tourist attractions, such as local festivals, museums, science centers, and parks.

72 – Travel your own Country (1991 to present)
We have made several trips within our country, in addition to the across Canada adventure, including multiple trips to New Brunswick and Montreal. We toured in Newfoundland when I was 17, performing in a band, for four weeks.

73 – Attend a Major Sporting Event (2012)
We took a family trip to the London summer Olympics, attending sporting events for rhythmic gymnastics, equestrian, and athletics. My daughter, Karah, helped qualify the Canadian National Rhythmic Gymnastics team for this event two years prior.

74 – FUTURE GOAL – to attend a major cultural event (TBD)

75 – Visit One of the 7 Wonders
I have visited the Golden Gate Bridge (CA), and the CN Tower (Toronto), multiple times, as well as the Roman Colosseum, in Italy (2016).

76 – Enjoy an All-Inclusive Vacation (1987–2016)
We've taken week-long vacations to resorts in Jamaica, Dominican Republic, Cuba (proposed to Kathy and got engaged in 1990), and Costa Rica.

77 – Take a Cruise Ship Vacation (2013 to present)
We've taken cruises to the Caribbean (2013), Bermuda (2015), Mediterranean (2016), and French Polynesia (2017). We are now planning for an Alaskan cruise.

78 – Go on an Island Vacation (2000 to present)
We have taken several island vacations, including to the Caribbean and to our absolute favourite island destination of Maui (7X).

79 – Experience an Entertainment City (1995 to present)
We have enjoyed entertainment travelling to Chicago, LA, New York City, Las Vegas, Orlando, and San Francisco. Our favourite experience was attending the "School of Rock" Broadway performance in Las Angeles in 2018.

80 – Travel the World (2003 to present) – Aruba, Bermuda, Bora Bora, Cuba, Costa Rica, Dominican Republic, France, Greece, Hawaii, Italy, Jamaica, Japan, Hong Kong, Tahiti, Thailand, Russia, Spain, UK, USA.

81 – Eat at Good Restaurants (2005 to present)
We've eaten at some of the best restaurants while on vacation, and while on date night, locally. We often seek out restaurants that have been featured on the TV show, *You've got to eat here!* Our greatest restaurant meal was at Mama's Fish House, on Maui, in 2017.

82 – Declutter your Life (2017)
We are just starting to enjoy the benefits of a decluttered house and life as a result of 3 things: our children growing up, building our dream house, and hiring a cleaner monthly. I'm continually thinking about how to purge things out of our life that are of limited use.

83 – Take Weekend Getaways (1991 to present)
Our favourite weekend getaway place is in Canada's prettiest town, Niagara On the Lake, for which we make annual getaways, usually around Christmas, our anniversary, or for birthdays. Also, we enjoy going to Niagara Falls and Toronto.

84 – Buy Quality Stuff (1991 to present)
I don't know exactly when we started, but it is important to us that we buy quality products at a reasonable price.

85 – Buy Our First House (1991)
Our first primary residence, a heritage century home, was purchased in 1991.

86 – Experience life (work in progress)

87 – Own or Have Access to a Vacation Property (2007)
We purchased our lakefront cottage on Lake Erie. We spend weekends at the cottage throughout the summer.

FUTURE OUTRAGEOUS GOAL – Tear down our existing cottage, and build our *dream cottage*. We are in discussions with an architect/designer now.

88 – Pay others to Do Chores (2014 to present)
There was a time, when we were starting out, where we'd do as much chore work as possible, including home renovations and maintenance. Now, more often than not, we pay professionals to do this work—like plumbers, carpenters, and cleaners.

89 – FUTURE GOAL – to own/drive my dream car (TBD)
When I was in my twenties, I had a dream to own a Mercedes 500SL two-door sports car. Now I vacillate between purchasing a variety of other sport/luxury vehicles—just a matter of time.

90 – Live in Your Dream House (2014)
We hired an amazing architect, contractor, and interior designer to custom design every aspect of our dream house, completing what was a 5-year project from initial design. We are thrilled to be living in our dream home, converting an 1886 heritage home into a spacious, updated space, while retaining its character and charm.
FUTURE GOAL – Tear down our garage, and rebuild with a *man cave* music room

91 – Keep a Life Journal (2016 to present)
I've been keeping journals and day timers, on and off, since 1991.

92 – FUTURE GOAL – to do something good for the world (TBD)
It is my hope that the writing of this book will lead to opportunities to help do something good in this world, as well as help people achieve their best life through living a goal-inspired life.

93 – Donate to Charity (2005 to present)
We have been donating to various charity groups for many years. The largest recipient of our donations, done through our work place, is the United Way campaign, which benefits local community groups in need of money. We've accomplished one of my original 100 goals: to give over $10,000 to charity (more to follow).

94 – FUTURE GOAL – to volunteer in your community (TBD)
In the writing of this book, I've been researching options for volunteer

opportunities in my own community. I have done some volunteering as part of our community's Sound of Music festival in recent years.

95 – FUTURE GOAL – to document my ancestry (TBD)
I've been archiving various historical evidence and documents related to my heritage; however, the goal to do this in a significant way lies ahead.

96 – Prepare Your Will (2005)
We last updated our will a while back, and we need to update again as things have changed within our financial life.

97 – Write a Book (2018)
If you are reading this book, I have achieved this goal! I also authored a second book published under The Authorities series entitled, *Buy Your Neighbours House,* for sale on Amazon.

98 – Document Your Life Story (2018)
I've journaled and tracked my life in various ways. The writing of this section on my own goal accomplishment is helping achieve this goal (more to come).

99 – FUTURE GOAL – to be a philanthropist and give over $1M away (TBD)

100 – FUTURE GOAL – to leave a financial inheritance (TBD)

WORDS OF WISDOM

If you've made it this far in this book, you've hopefully been inspired to **write down the goals** that you'd like to achieve. The challenge for you (and me) is that goal achievement is a long-term deal. If you set this book aside and move to your next book or some project demanding your attention, it will be easy to leave this behind. My suggestion to you is that you commit to reading this book once a year, at one of two times: leading up to your birthday, or leading up to December 31st, the end of the calendar year.

Staying focused on reading self-help books is the biggest piece of advice I can give you. Also, check out my website, **www.100GoalsClub.com**, for information on how you can stay in contact with me and be part of a club committed to goal achievement.

YOUR PERSONALIZED LIST OF GOALS

Personal Development

_____
_____
_____
_____
_____
_____
_____
_____
_____
_____
_____

Health and Fitness

_____
_____
_____
_____
_____
_____
_____
_____
_____

Family and Friends

_____
_____
_____
_____
_____
_____
_____
_____
_____
_____

Hobbies and Passions

_____
_____
_____
_____
_____
_____
_____
_____
_____
_____
_____

Financial

_____
_____
_____
_____
_____
_____
_____
_____
_____

Career

_____
_____
_____
_____
_____
_____
_____
_____
_____
_____

Adventure

_____
_____
_____
_____
_____
_____
_____
_____
_____
_____

Travel

_____
_____
_____
_____
_____
_____
_____
_____
_____

Lifestyle

_____
_____
_____
_____
_____
_____
_____
_____
_____
_____

Giving Back / Leave a Legacy

Made in the USA
Monee, IL
21 January 2022

89550288R00115